Chinese Folk Embroidery

Wang Yarong

Thames and Hudson

First published in Great Britain in 1987 by Thames and Hudson Ltd, London

Author: Wang Yarong
Managing Editor: Chan Man Hung
Executive Editor: Yim Lai Kuen
Arts Co-ordinators: Wan Yat Sha Yau Pik Shan
Arts Editor: Wan Yat Sha
Designers: Yau Pik Shan Wan Yat Sha

Printed and bound in Hongkong by C & C Joint Printing Co., (H.K.) Ltd.

Contents

Notes on the list of pictures

This list with page numbers provided is compiled for quick reference.

Pictures in three categories are included in this book:

(1) Plates (numbered 1, 2, 3 . . .)
(2) Illustrations (numbered "Illustration no.1", "Illustration no.2", and so on)
(3) Illustrations showing various embroidering techniques (numbers in italics)

Unless otherwise stated, the pictures are all furnished by the author and the Research Group of Dress and Ornaments of the Research Institute of History affiliated to the Chinese Academy of Social Science.

List of pictures

(I) Plates

(A) Accessories

(B) Designs on Clothes

(C) Embroidered Household Articles

(D) Designs in Chinese Embroidery

(2) Illustrations

(3) Illustrations Showing Various Embroidering Techniques

1. THE DEVELOPMENT OF CHINESE FOLK EMBROIDERY

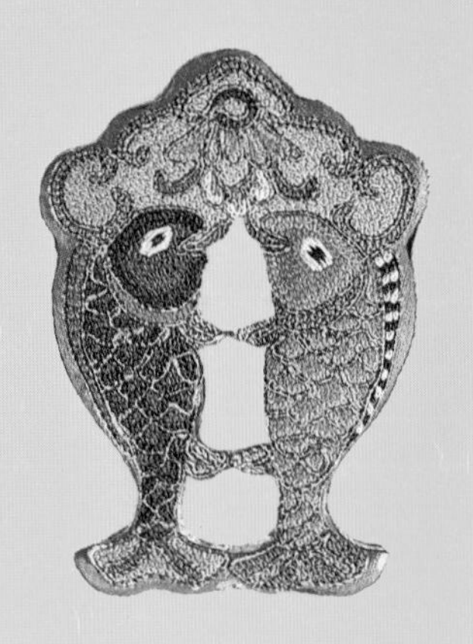

(I)

Embroidery, popularly known as *xiuhua* or *zhahua* (both meaning making ornamental designs in cloth with a needle), is one of the finest Chinese national arts. The characters *jin* (brocade) and *xiu* (embroidery) have been used together from time immemorial by the Chinese to describe splendid or exquisite things — for instance, a land of incomparable beauty, a promising future, or wit. However, the design on brocade and the pattern on embroidery are formed quite differently: the former is made by the method of *tihua* or warp-lifting on the loom, while the latter is made on finished fabrics by using needles and coloured silk threads in accordance with designed patterns and by the application of various stitching techniques. (1) Needles and threads are to a skilled embroidery artist what brush, ink and colours are to a painter. As every age boasted its famous artists, they must have left behind a considerable quantity of embroidered works; of these, however, only a few have been handed down owing to the perishable nature of silk goods, and these are now being carefully kept by collectors in China and abroad.

The art of embroidery has a long history in China. The historical records of the Qin dynasty mention things like "embroidered robes and undergarments", "imperial robes and embroidered undergarments", as well as "white robes embroidered with red designs". (2) *Shang Shu*, a history book of an earlier period, in its *Book of Yu*, told the story of how Shun, the legendary emperor, ordered Yu to make clothes: "I want to see the pictures done by the ancients: those drawn in imitation of the sun, the moon, stars, mountain, dragon and pheasant as well as those embroidered in the forms of ritual wine vessels, aquatic plants, fire, white rice and the designs of *fu* (patterns in black and white colours) and *fu* (patterns in black and blue colours). These are to be in brilliant colours and added to dyed cloth to make garments." This was, in fact, the celebrated official costume in twelve colours worn by the Son of Heaven (emperor). (3) Ancient monarchs usually wore an upper garment decorated with paintings in six colours and a lower garment ornamented with embroidered designs, also in six colours. This system of dress was esteemed as a sacred institution and passed from generation to generation until the end of the Qing dynasty. Yuan Shiai, who sought to restore the monarchy after the founding of the Republic, also took great interest in reviving the use of this official costume.

Though multicoloured figured brocade became popular in the Spring-and-Autumn and Warring States periods, (4) it could not compare with embroidery in artistic appeal, and this was particularly true where large-scale designs were concerned. Moreover, the upper echelons still put a premium on clothes with designs either painted or embroidered on them, owing to the difficulty of the techniques involved in their making and the restrictions of tradition. In the meantime, the art of embroidery gradually attained perfection, a fact borne out by the precious relics excavated in recent decades. The earliest proofs are the traces of embroidered rhombic designs on a Shang bronze wine vessel, (5) and the impression of embroidered work executed in Chain Stitch found in a Western Zhou tomb at Rujiazhuang, Baoji, Shanxi Province (6) (Illustration No.1). Later examples are the embroidered pieces of silk found in a Huang (name of a state) tomb dating from the early Spring-and-Autumn period, situated at Guangshan, Xinyang, Henan Province (Illustration No.2); a phoenix-design embroidered work of Eastern Zhou unearthed in the Soviet Union; (7) and the fragment of phoenix-pattern embroidery found in a Chu tomb in Changsha, Hunan Province. (8) Particularly noteworthy are the embroidered clothes and bedding of the middle and late Warring States Period (between the fourth and the third centuries BC) discovered in No.1 Chu tomb at Mashan, Jiangling, Hubei Province in early 1982 (9) (Illustration Nos. 3, 4). The good condition in which they are preserved, their beautiful colours, the diversity of the patterns, boldly and ingeniously designed, and the lively and flowing artistic styles, are the qualities that place them far above all the previously known specimens. The techniques involved in their making have indeed attained a very high level, through which the artists have incorporated ornamental as well as utilitarian features.

Of the embroideries made in the two Han dynasties, which belonged to a somewhat later period, even more specimens have been found. The most typical are the findings from No.1 and No.3 Han tombs at Mawangdui, Changsha, Hunan Province, and many of these embroidered works have been preserved intact (10) (Illustration No. 5). In spite of their beauty and elegance, the designs can hardly match those of the Warring States Period in splendour. The patterns are smaller in size, and are practically indistinguishable from the designs of the embroideries in Chain Stitch found in the northwest and datable to the same period. This suggests the production of a standardized commodity in a unified country under the rule of the Qin and Han imperial governments. (11) An embroidered work with tiny flowers with stems as its motif, discovered in a Western Han tomb in Jiangling (Illustration No.6), may represent a more popular design congenial to the taste of the common people. Specimens of the two Han dynasties have also been discovered in Beijing (Dabaotai), Gansu (Wuwei), Shanxi (Huaian), Xinjiang (Niya and

1. The impression of embroidered work in Chain Stitch found in a West Zhou tomb at Rujiazhuang, Baoji, Shaanxi Province

2. Fragment of embroidered work in Chain Stitch found in a tomb of the State of Huang (dating from the early Spring-and-Autumn Period) at Guangshan, Xinyang, Henan Province

3. Tiger design embroidered in Chain Stitch, found in a Chu tomb at Mashan, Jiangling, Hubei Province

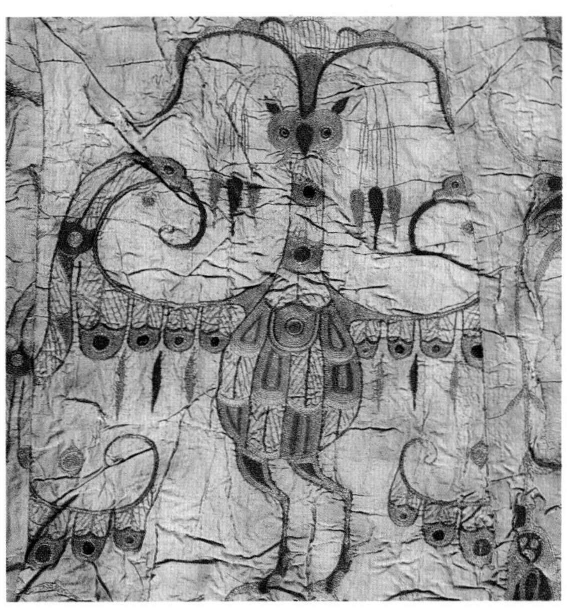

4. Design of bird embroidered in Chain Stitch, found in a Chu tomb at Mashan, Jiangling, Hubei Province

5. Design symbolizing longevity embroidered in Chain Stitch, found in No. 1 West Han tomb at Mawangdui, Changsha, Hunan Province

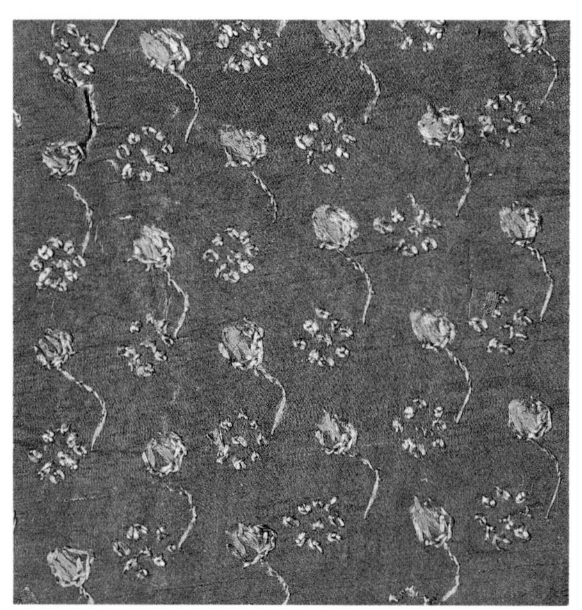

6. Designs of tiny flowers embroidered in Chain Stitch, found in a West Han tomb at Fenghuangshan, Jiangling, Hubei Province

7. Designs embroidered with Single Close-knit Stitch, found in No. I Han tomb at Mawangdui, Changsha, Hunan Province

8. Appliqué work with silk and feathers, found in No. I Han tomb at Mawangdui, Changsha, Hunan Province

9. Facsimile of an embroidered piece unearthed in Xinjiang (painted by Wang Xu)

Luobunaoer) and places beyond the national frontier (Pamila and Nuoyinwula). (12) They help to throw new light on the embroidering art of two thousand years ago.

Technically speaking, most of the above-mentioned specimens are executed in Chain Stitch. The lines formed by joining tiny rings of silk thread can be used to make all sorts of patterns. For more than 1700 years, between the Shang dynasty and the last years of the Eastern Han dynasty, the Chain Stitch always played a predominant role. Designs, whether formed by coloured lines or patches, are universally embroidered with Chain Stitch and only with rare exceptions are Satin Stitches used instead (Illustration No.7).

The varieties of Chain Stitch are the Open-ring Stitch, the Close-ring Stitch, the Braid Stitch, the Loop Stitch, the Daisy Stitch, the Fly Stitch and Consecutive Stitch (Split Stitch), the last of these being easier to execute but producing almost the same effect as the Chain Stitch itself. The Loop Stitch and the Daisy Stitch are usually used to form dots and strokes, while the Consecutive Stitch is employed to delineate the thin end of a fine line. Among the specimens of the Western Han, embroideries were also found exhibiting use of other techniques, such as the Satin Stitch, the Knot Stitch and the addition of exotic materials such as silk or feathers (13) (Illustration No.8). The commencement of the Jin and Southern and Northern Dynasties saw rapid development of the use of the Satin Stitch because of the growing need to embroider the images of Buddha, human faces, lilies, peonies, and mandarin ducks in their natural forms. This technique reached full maturity after the Sui and the Tang dynasties, and thereafter a new period began in which could be seen the mixed use of various skills and their development.

Judging from the evolution and progress of the art of stitchery, we can be sure that embroidery in its early stages was meant to serve a practical purpose. But the art could not be fully developed until the materials suitable for embroidering made their appearance. The practice of adorning clothes with painted or embroidered designs might well be an extension of the custom of tattooing prevalent amongst primitive people. Being simpler in technique than figure-weaving, embroidery skills proved capable of being popularized at a time when material resources were extremely limited, and among the skills available, people naturally chose products that could turn out both durable and useful. In this respect, chain stitching is far superior to satin stitching, which accounts for the former method being so widely used during that long period.

It was long, long afterwards that the embroidering skills which produced objects for display and admiration began to emerge. During the Northern and Southern Dynasties, however, people began to embroider images of Buddha, and then the flower-and-bird painting style which came to maturity in the succeeding Song dynasty lent itself to the further development of these skills.

Religious subjects and images of birds and flowers embroidered in Even Stitches, Winding Stitches and Close-knit Stitches (which all belong to the category of the Satin Stitch), are commonly seen on the relics of Tang. The artists at that time were already proficient in using the Layered Short-straight Stitch to create related colours in graduated tones in order to achieve the effect of shading (Illustration No.9). By that time, the *ping-jin* method (gluing a piece of gold foil on sheepskin or paper and then cutting this into thin strips to be used in embroidering) had already developed. The object described by the Tang poet Bai Juyi as being decorated with strips of gold and strings of pearls must have been made by this method. The embroidered works discovered in a Liao (a dynasty established by a nomadic people called Qidan) tomb, built about AD 960 and situated at Yemaotai, Faku, Liaoning Province, show that the skills we have just described continued to play a major role, with the Tang style predominating in embroidering deer and flowers, as these were all done with Winding Stitches, supplemented by Consecutive Stitches and Couching here and there. A small scent-bag was even adorned with silver-and-gold-foil strips to achieve a perfect harmony between the skills used and the creative effect which the artist sought to produce (Illustrations Nos.10, 11).

In the later period of the Northern Song dynasty an imperial embroidery workshop was set up in the capital, which employed three hundred embroiderers and supplied the court with products both for daily usage and display. The "embroidered paintings" and the "embroidered calligraphies" which they produced under the influence of the academic school of painting became very popular. During the succeeding dynasties of Southern Song and Yuan, the intellectuals who either served in the government or lived in retirement in the country helped to develop a *literati* culture in the south. Under their patronage a new school of embroidering art, excelling in embroidering pictures and calligraphies purely for visual display, was formed. As it grew farther and farther away from the popular form of embroidery, it gradually became one with painting, devoting itself to the production of works of art after the models supplied by painters and calligraphers like Huang Quan, Cui Bai, Su Shi, Mi Fu and others. In order to achieve the effect of ink and brush so that the embroidered works would appear just like the originals, it was necessary to devise new techniques in stitchery and colour-blending, thereby stimulating innovations and improvements in the art of satin stitching. The Southern Song embroidered painting *Riding a Crane over a Beautiful Terrace* (Illustration No.12) based on a picture by a famous artist, for example, was made using no less than fifteen different skills, including the Even Stitch, the Mixed Straight Stitch, Darning, the Stern Stitch, the Consecutive Stitch, the Knot Stitch, the Net Stitch, the Pine-needle Stitch, the Random Stitch, Couching, and the use of gold accents and colours to supplement the stitching. It is truly a representative work as far as stitchwork and colour-blending are concerned. But when we compare these skills with ones used in making the everyday objects unearthed from Huang Sheng's tomb (Southern Song) in Fuzhou, (14) we can see they are practically the same, a fact testifying to the high level of the folk embroidery art of the time, and giving rise to the conjecture that the skills used by the school of "embroidered painting" were actually derived from the humbler but more popular form of embroidery. Other examples are the Southern Song embroideries found in Shanxi. Among the techniques used are Gauze-embroidering and *Chuosha* (both resembling *petit point* in the West) besides satin stitching. These two methods are capable of achieving a strong decorative effect. They exerted a profound influence on the development of some skills used in the later Suzhou embroidery after they became popular. These examples illustrate the fact that a growing repertoire of popular embroidery techniques paved the way for the technical development of a more sophisticated branch of the art.

The Yuan rulers showed particular interest in embroidered works adorned with gold. As there was a government-run embroidery factory employing women to make a variety of items for daily use, much progress must have been made in the use of gold. Unfortunately few specimens of the time are now in existence. However, we can still gain some insight into the achievement made in that dynasty through a Yuan embroidery entitled *Lotus Sutra* and another, *Prajnaparamita Sutra*, now preserved by the Liaoning Provincial Museum (Illustration No.13). The unique feature of the second work consists in the use of single threads to delineate the outlines of the images in imitation of the Song painter Li Gonglin's strokes, as well as in the patterns which decorate the clothes worn by the holy personages, as they are done with various kinds of Net stitches, a well-developed skill which had established itself as an independent form by then.

Inspired by the experiences of Song and Yuan artists, the Gu family living at Luxiangyuan, Jiangsu Province in the last years of Ming, specialized in embroidering pictures after famous artists and succeeded in leading the fashion and taste of the time. Though they achieved less than they have been credited with, they did succeed in advancing the skills of Song and Yuan. The *Maitreya* they embroidered is wearing a robe adorned with extremely complex designs. He is shown sitting on a hassock made of cat-tails. The artist seemed to have gone too far in an effort to imitate reality. At the same time, influenced by the use of extremely fine lines to outline human figures by the *literati* painter You Qiu, they initiated "hair embroidery" (15) in which new-born babies' hair was used. This entitled them to occupy a niche in the development of stitching techniques.

The above-mentioned kind of embroidery made little impression on the common folk, who needed embroideries which could serve both practical and ornamental purposes. However, satin stitching developed by the artists of the more sophisticated branch of embroidery, when absorbed by artisans, did add to the rich repertoire of skills already in their possession.

In the early stage of Qing, with the revival of the national economy, a handicraft textile industry engaged in the production of household articles began to thrive on the foundations already laid down during the Ming dynasty. Local embroidery products of Suzhou, Guangdong, Sichuan and Hunan appeared and competed in the market. As embroidering techniques kept improving and the dress of the upper classes became more and more luxurious, for a time the costly method of split-colour-floss embroidering was universally adopted. Commercial houses, which went by the name of "Gu's embroidery shop", were set up in the cities to trade in embroidered goods and thereby meet the market demand. They took orders and sold all sorts of embroideries: things to be given as gifts, theatrical costumes and embroideries for ornamental purposes, daily use and export. As there was an increasing demand for embroideries in everyday life, more and more families began to produce them. Products with local features could be found all over the country. Of these, the most famous ones were those made in Suzhou, Guangdong, Sichuan and Hunan. Next in order of achievement were those made in Beijing, Shanghai, Shandong, Hangzhou, Wenzhou, Fujian and Kaifeng. There were also embroidered works produced by minority peoples in the northwest and southwest of China, such as the Miao, the Mongolians, the Uygurs, the Yi, the Li, the Aini and others, who with their different historical background and traditions, besides making special textiles for consumption at home, also produced a great variety of exquisite and useful embroideries with a charm of their own.

Many and varied were the methods involved in stitching and in the dyeing and splitting of silk-floss. It goes without saying that stitching is the most fundamental skill in embroidery. Many embroidering artists and connoisseurs have tried to make a systematic study of the skills. But as there are so many of them, it is

10. Embroidered scented bag found in a Liao tomb at Yemaotai, Liaoning Province

12. Southern Song embroidered painting *Riding a Crane Over a Beautiful Terrace* (preserved by the Liaoning Provincial Museum)

11. Part of an embroidered cap found in a Liao tomb at Yemaotai, Liaoning Province

13. Image of Buddha executed with Net Stitch in a Yuan embroidered painting (preserved by the Liaoning Provincial Museum)

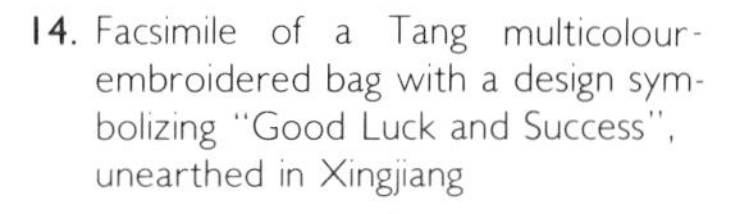

14. Facsimile of a Tang multicolour-embroidered bag with a design symbolizing "Good Luck and Success", unearthed in Xingjiang

impossible to include every technique in use, and consequently only the most important ones are mentioned here (See also: Part III of this book): the Chain Stitch, the Knot Stitch, the Satin Stitch, the Piling Method, *Chuosha*, Gauze-embroidering, Knitting, the Net Stitch, Darning, *Guarong* (wool-scraping), *Gerong* (wool-cutting), Drawn-work, *pantiao* (coiling of strings), the Pulling Stitch, Pearl Threading, *Tiaohua* (picking patterns), Carving Method, Blanket Stitch, *Tiejuan* (applique), Couching, *Quanjin* (circling with gold), *Pingjin* and Gold-shadowing Embroidery. The prosperous reigns of Kangxi, Yongzheng and Qianlong (1661-1796), comparatively speaking, were a period of social stability and peace.

Embroidering had become a universal pastime for women, who practised it all their lives. As a result, " even the dullest ones became expert and practice made perfect", thereby ushering in a period of full bloom for the art, with a stunning array of skills and products that competed with each other.

(II)

The plates contained in this book chiefly represent small and sundry embroidered ornaments for wearing, made after the seventeeth century. They include ornamental collars, cuffs, bags of various shapes and sizes (scent-bags, fan cases, small bags, spectacle cases, mirror cases, key cases, scissors cases), pin cushions, and pouches for tailor's chalk lines. There are also a few samples of embroidered works made by minority groups, which show strong ethnic features. Besides those made for sale by artisans of the bag shops, most of the specimens were made by women at home to be used as ornaments or given as gifts to close relations on special occasions. They differ vastly in style, depending on when and where these embroideries were made as well as on the racial background of the craftspeople.

Meriting particular attention are the sundry embroidered objects hung at the waist, (16) such as scent-bags, pouches, and fan cases. They were worn by all, irrespective of their age, sex, rank or race, and were therefore one of the most typical kind of accessories made by folk embroiderers. First contrived to meet some practical need, their origin can be traced far back into antiquity.

The custom of carrying a bag to hold sundry things one needed constantly, or a bag filled with fragrant materials, began as early as the Shang and Zhou dynasties. Among the funerary objects discovered in the tombs built at that time were pin-cases and knives, which people hung at the waist in ancient times. The earliest record of this custom can be found in *Li Ji*, a book written in the Han dynasty. In its section dealing with rules of domestic conduct, it says that in the days of Qin men wore leather *pan* and women wore silk *pan*, which was later described by Zheng Xuan of the Eastern Han dynasty as a small bag to hold towels. The bag, made of leather or silk, was usually painstakingly decorated. The book also names a dozen or so objects which a son should carry with him in order to serve his parents. These included towels, knives, whetstones, awls for undoing knots, fire-making tools and other items. In the same way, a woman was required to carry sewing implements like needles and threads contained in an embroidered bag in order to serve her husband's parents. Young people of both sexes who had not come of age were obliged to wear a scent-bag to show respect for their seniors. (17) As these small bags were constantly carried, both for practical needs and for decoration, people spared no pains to have them finely made and ornamented. There were also fixed rules governing the way to wear them. The book's account is perhaps the earliest record of these objects worn at the waist.

From the relics found in the Han tomb at Mawangdui, it can be seen that the scent-bag of the time consisted of a body, a top, a bottom, a neck and a string to close the opening with. It was usually made of high-quality silk and contained fragrant plants (18) both for scenting clothes and carrying about. If we compare it with the scent-bags described in the famous Han poem *The Peacock Flying to the Southeast,* which were attached to the four corners of a mosquito net, we can see that it could not be used as a hanging ornament. It might resemble the early Tang scent-bag unearthed in Xinjiang (Illustration No.14). Mentioning the ranks of military officers, an Eastern Han record describes an "embroidered bag with the design of tiger-head" worn on one side of the waist that went by the name of "side bag" or "ribbon bag", for it contained the ribbon attached to the official seal. We can gain a clearer idea of this type of bag by comparing the description with the stone-carving discovered in a Han tomb at Yinan, Shandong Province, which depicts a military man carrying such a bag (19) (Illustration No.15). It is clear that the embroidery at this time was executed by means of Chain Stitches. In the *History of the Three Kingdoms,* Cao Cao, the founder of the Wei dynasty, was described as "dressed in light silk and wearing a small bag to hold towels and sundry things". In early Tang it became a rule for one to carry on one's person seven objects (20) similar to those carried by the people in ancient times. In the Song, Yuan, Liao and Jin dynasties, the nomadic peoples of the north were known for their custom of carrying a bag, which contained a flint, a knife and a whetstone (Illustration No.16).

During the two hundred years and more of the Qing dynasty, embroidered bags hung at the waist were much in vogue (Illustration No.17). A complete set of these hanging ornaments was popularly called "court-style nine objects". This situation was the result of the influence exerted by the ruling ethnic groups — the Manchurians and the Mongolians — who were at the top of social scale but still adhered to their old customs. Moreover, peace and order throughout the land proved beneficial to the development of a handicraft industry, which in turn enabled the nobility to live in comfort and luxury and vie with one another in displaying their wealth by means of dress and ornament. Embroidered objects for decorative purposes were given as presents by the court as well as by officials among themselves. They became indispensable items in the course of social interaction. Taking the example of scent-bags, *Gu Wan Zhi Nan Xu Bian* (the sequel to *A Guide to Collectors of Antiques)* says: "People in all walks of life — rich or poor, of noble or common birth — wore scent-bags in summer. They were obtainable in every corner of the capital city. Even more numerous were the bags offered for sale at the fair and market-place (Illustration No.18). In those days, a man would be thought untidily dressed if he failed to carry a scent-bag on a hot day, thus causing pain to himself and the censure of the public. People attached so much importance to them that even the lower strata spared no pains to procure them. Every skill used in embroidery was employed to embellish the object so much sought after and the rich took pride in the extremely fine fancy works in their possession." The bags took different forms, but in the city the most popular ones were those shaped like a chicken-heart, an ellipse or gourd. Let us quote a few verses from the poems written in the middle and late Qing, which satirize the abuse of the time by mentioning the embroidered small bags. The first example is the *Poem After the Bamboo Twig Pattern** composed by Yang Miren (taken from the edition of 1796):

Suishang piao makes finest pipes,
Zierbenzhi made of fine jade.
Knotting and use of gold accent are all the go,
And the Hui** bags tied with silk threads. (21)

The next example is De Shuoting's poem entitled *A String of Rough Pearls* (written during the reign of Jiaqing). It reads:

Knotting, *pingjin* and appliqué
are not much to brag about,
Just see how many womenfolk
spend their time on *Chuosha*.

Such poems are too numerous to cite. We learn from them the fashion of that period as well as the fact that not only the shapes of the bags but also the skills involved in their making changed constantly. For instance, the Knot Stitch and the use of gold accent were popular in the last years of Qianlong (around 1795), but during the reign of Jiaqing (1796-1820) *Chuosha* (jabbing the fabric) seemed to gain public favour; which, however, returned to *dazi* and *pingjin* later on. The poems also tell us that these fine works of art were mostly made by women of the humbler families.

In the city, women used very small bags which were usually exquisitely made. Some wore around their body one or two scent-bags, silver tweezers, a silver earpick and the like — "three silver things" or "seven silver things". Women from aristocratic families often had them made of gold and set with jewels to display their wealth (Illustration No.19).

These small-size embroideries elaborately made by folk embroiderers, with the exception of a negligible quantity sold as merchandise to commercial houses, were not for sale. They were used as gifts on such occasions as wed-

* This is one of the set patterns in Chinese poetry.

** "Hui" refers to the Uygur people in Xinjiang.

15. Stone-carving in a Han tomb found in Yinan, Shandong Province, depicting a military man carrying a bag embroidered with a tiger-head

16. A Yuan tomb mural found in Chifeng, Inner Mongolia, depicting a man carrying a bag

17. A picture entitled *The Empress Dowager Playing Chess* showing players wearing bags and thumb-rings

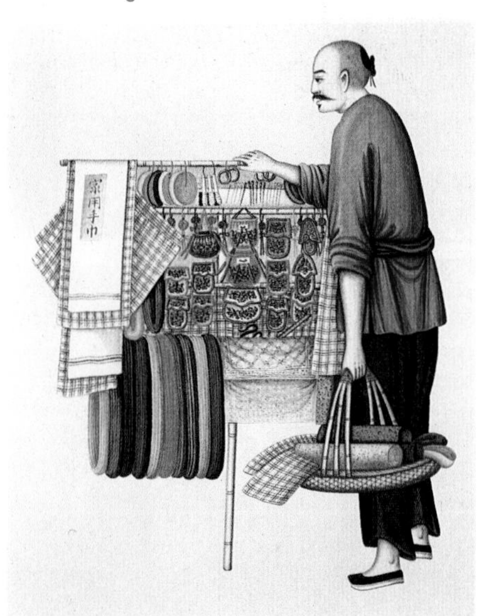

18. Late Qing Dynasty painting, showing a bag-peddler in Guangdong

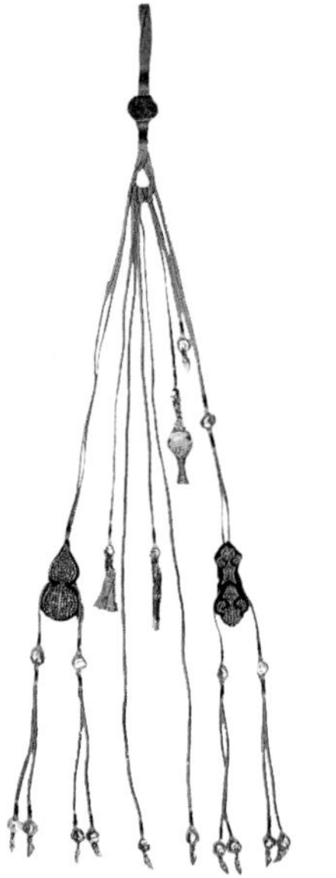

19. Bags embroidered with pearls worn on the chest by women of rank. These were unearthed from the tomb of an imperial princess in Chifeng

dings and festival celebrations. Miniature umbrellas, fans, clothes and shoes of extremely fine workmanship dedicated to gods represented another variety.

Some fifty or sixty years ago, in the rural areas of North China, girls began learning needlework and embroidery at the age of six or seven. They gradually perfected their skills as they grew up. When they reached a marriageable age, they had to prepare a considerable number of tiny embroidered bags of all shapes. Besides the common shapes of chicken-heart, gourd and ellipse, the bags also took the form of flower baskets, seedpods of the lotus, silver ingots, lanterns, doublefishes, double-coins, and *zong* (somewhat resembling a quadrilateral pyramid) wound with colour threads. All these suggest auspiciousness and were further adorned with hanging loops, decorative knots or tassels made of coloured silk threads. The tiny pieces of embroidery were then strung together and put into baskets made of coloured straw in the shape of flowers or fruits, with the first piece of a string fixed on the cover of the basket. On the day of the wedding, when friends and relatives crowded in to have a look at the dowry of the bride, they would see strings of beautifully made tiny bags contained in the baskets, giving convincing evidence of her skill and cleverness. She would then present these specially made bags to her female relatives of older generations, such as her mother-in-law, and the more elderly friends, as well as her new sisters-in-law. In anticipation of the happy event, usually twelve pairs (and, in the case of rich families, one hundred pairs) of embroidered shoes were made. As both the Chinese characters standing for "shoe" and "together" are pronounced *xie*, a pun could thus be formed to mean that the newly married couple would live together to a great age.

The Ornamental collar evolving from the "robe of feathers" of Sui was quite fashionable amongst the nobility during the Yuan dynasty. Worn by both men and women, it was in the shape of four *ruyi* (S-shape) joined together, a pattern that influenced the decoration of porcelain vases of later periods. In the Qing dynasty, the collar became an article of clothing worn by all, especially young women. It generally had two layers made of eight parts, each embroidered with pictures based on some popular plays, or designs of flowers and insects. One elaborately made collar took six to twelve months to complete. Full of the spirit of emulation, young women usually did their best in an attempt to beat others. This was particularly so with a bride, who must put on finery made with her own hands to call on her relations during the first Lunar New Year after her marriage. This of course afforded chances for mutual learning. It goes without saying that embroidered works produced under such circumstances must be full of originality and life, not to be matched by those made and sold as commodities or those which slavishly imitated the works of painters or calligraphers.

(III)

Historically speaking, though embroidery and brocade had been placed on a par since ancient times, the former, being free from the restrictions imposed by the loom, enjoyed a number of advantages: the wide range of its themes, the great variety of designs in which full scope could be given to the display of personality and, in particular, its complicated colour schemes. All this enabled it to exert an influence over the latter in artistic expression. For example, the *rongguanjin* or pile-loop brocade of the Western Han was clearly in imitation of the then-existing chain embroidery with raised loop patterns. (22) The "shading" technique in weaving most probably originated from the use of a striated mixture of colours to create a feeling of wash in satin stitching. The skill was perhaps adopted by weavers before the Sui and Tang dynasties. Its influence on the later ages was evidenced by such products as *yunjianjin* of Tang, *dabaozhaojin* and *badayunjin* of Song, which were all woven with the technique of " shading", as well as by the skill of creating wash in colour wall-paintings in the Song and Ming dynasties. (23) The *zhuanghua* or patterned brocade of Ming might be something fashioned after the then popular *Chuosha* embroidery. At the same time, it also applied the *kesi* (weft-woven silk) technique of weaving colour weft threads, each on a separate bobbin, to form designs that looked as beautiful as embroidery, while the warp (brocade) ground, which did not mix with the colour weft threads, was extremely harmonious and clear in colour.

As far as designs are concerned, the miscellaneous embroidered bags, though small in size, have a great variety of themes: landscapes, trees, flowers, the sun, the moon, clouds, gardens, animals, insects, characters from famous stories, geometric patterns, auspicious symbols and so on, in fact, almost everything under the sun. Moreover, the compositions are well conceived; the stitching techniques are many and varied; the skills to achieve harmony or contrast in colour, in particular, lend additional charm to the designs. Indeed, these skills embody the wisdom and achievement of a very high order left behind by our ancestors. They represent a heritage worthy of careful study and imitation.

The colours used in folk embroidery pose a difficult problem. Generally speaking, items used on happy occasions like New Year, weddings and birthdays are embroidered in strongly contrasting rich colours. Items for ordinary use are usually in light, soft and subtle colours. Sometimes they are only slightly touched with colours to impress one with their quiet beauty. The embroideries of the south are of fine workmanship, pretty in colour and full of vitality; those of the north, crude, simple and regular in patterns and solemn in colour; the artists of Guangdong, a seaside province, with a style all their own, prefer a warm and bold colour scheme uninhibited by tradition; the extensive and dreary grasslands and deserts of the northwest are sparsely inhabited by a migrating population, who are in favour of vivid colours to offset the dullness of their natural environment as well as to bring out the vastness and distance before their eyes, an effect almost unbearable to a city dweller living in cramped conditions. (Similarly the costumes of the Peking opera are embroidered with patterns in rich colours so that they can be seen clearly at a distance.) As hand-made products gradually drop out of everyday life with the development of modern industry, many people falsely believe that folk embroiderers use only loud colours. In fact, the chromatic schemes used by embroiderers are really extremely extensive. The names of a great many colours can be found in various records of Song, Yuan and later ages, (24) though these only represent a fraction of the colours in use, for it is said that in late Qing period, several hundred different colours were actually used by the handicraft dyers throughout the country. There were, for example, no less than thirty shades of brown. *Xue Huan Xiu Pu*, a book devoted to the art of embroidery, says that the number of colours used in embroidery amounts to eighty-eight, with a total of 745 different shades. A tiny piece of embroidery is usually executed in ten or more colours. Though polychrome threads are capable of forming vivid and glorious pictures, monochrome threads, on the other hand, can be manipulated to present an effect of shade; and the designs thus formed can be both calm and elegant. No matter what monochrome threads one uses — crimson, deep blue, or black on a white ground; white on a blue ground; white, blue, or black on a scarlet ground; white or red on a green ground — the patterns made can be either calm or sumptuous with the proper selection of designs (simple or complicated, densely or thinly distributed). (25) Attempts to embroider shiny patterns on a deep darkish (sometimes on a fresh green) ground have succeeded in creating striking and admirable effects.

With small-size embroideries, tiny designs faintly touched with colours are usually embroidered on a light coloured ground and large designs in rich colours on a deeply coloured ground. But this is by no means a hard and fast rule. Adding borders to the designs, leaving out narrow spaces between the embroidered patterns (voiding) and using gold or silver accents are the methods employed to soften strong contrast in colour. Folk embroiderers are also good at the skill of "shading" to achieve harmony between colours. There was, in fact, a widely used series of colour-blending skills in Chinese traditional weaving and embroidering arts. The word "shading" means the use of graduated tones of the same colour or related colours to achieve harmony or the effect of wash. There is still a formula for colour-blending datable to Ming and Qing passed by word of mouth among the handicraft weavers of the *Zhuanghua* brocade. (26) The formula consists of two parts — the "blending of two colours" and the "blending of three colours".

Blending of two colours:
jade white and blue
feather grey and blue
sunflower yellow and green
ancient bronze and purple
crimson and pink
and others.

Blending of three colours:
sunflower yellow, green and azurite
cerise, pale rose and deep red
jade white, pale blue and sapphire blue
qiuxiang (greenish yellow), bronze and snuff
silvery grey, tile grey and pigeon grey
deep and light bronzes and camel
date dark brown, grape and bronze
and others.

The formula does not include everything and is subject to alteration. It is unfortunate that a more complete knowledge of the techniques involved is not possible.

Moreover, records of colour-blending in folk embroidery can also be found in Ming and Qing novels like *Jin Ping Mei* and *A Dream of Red Mansions*. Chapter 35 of *A Dream of Red Mansions* tells how a maid made a net for her young master Baoyu; reflecting the general tendency of the time, it includes a discussion on the question of colour-blending.

Another matter of note is that dyers at that time used only natural dyes yielded by plants. This accounts for the fact that the age-old embroideries made with silk threads dyed in this way can still retain their rich, mellow, brilliant and yet elegant colours after so many years. Natural dyes have been used for several thousand years and a complete process has been developed for their manufacture and application. On the other hand, the use of synthesized organic dyes, (27) dating from their invention by W.H. Perkin in 1856, has a history of little more than one hundred years. So we have yet much to learn from our ancestors about the matching, setting-off and mixing of colours as well as the handling of the overall effect, when embroidering with threads treated with modern dyes.

The designs, the workmanship and the pattern of colour distribution of a good piece of embroidery usually embody the wisdom, labour and feelings of generations of women. The embroiderers have indeed accumulated much experience and knowledge in pattern-designing and colour-blending. When we view the works that have come down to us from past generations, we cannot help noticing that those done in simple chromatic schemes do not appear monotonous at all, while the multicolour ones never fail to impress one with their neatness. The great diversity of skills and colours used are all regulated by some traditional rules and help to shape a style at once robust, cheerful, charming and splendid.

Notes

1. Xia Nai: Archaeology and History of Science and Technology (Beijing, Ke Xue Publishing House, 1979). P.86.
2. These examples are found in the following parts of the *Book of Songs: Qin Folksong - Zhongnan Bin Folksong-jiuyu* (net made of rope) and *Tang Folksong - Small Creek*. As to the question of embroidering with threads dyed red, the reader can refer to Wang Xu's "The Designs on Silk Fabrics Unearthed in a Han Tomb at Mawangdui", *Archaeological Researches* (no.5, 1979). P.447
3. According to *Tong Dian* (by Du You), all the designs adopted had their connotations. The sun, the moon and the stars stood for the shedding of light; the mountain for heaviness; the dragon for change; the pheasant for beautiful designs; ancestral wine vessels for filial piety; water plants for purity; fire for brightness; rice for nourishment; the design of *fu* (in the shape of an axe) for sharpness; the design of *fu* (in the shape of two Chinese characters *yi* or *gong* arranged back to back) for distinctiveness.
4. Xiong Chuanxin: "Silk Fabrics of the Warring States Period Recently Found in Changsha", *Cultural Relics* (No.2, 1975). Chen Yuejun and Zhan Xuqiu: Silk Fabrics of the Warring States Period Unearthed from No.1 Chu Tomb at Mazhuan, Jiangling," *Cultural Relics* (No.10, 1982).
5. Vivi Sylwan: "Silk from the Yin Dynasty", *The Museum of Far Eastern Antiquities* (Bulletin No.9, 1937, Stockholm). P.123-124.
6. Li Yezhen, et. al.: "An Important Discovery Concerning the Silk Weaving and Embroidery of the Western Zhou", *Cultural Relics* (No.4, 1976), Plate I.
7. Commission for the Preservation of Historical Relics of Xinyang District, Henan Province and the Cultural Centre of Guangshan County: "Report on the Excavation of the Tomb of Huang Junmeng and His Wife, Who Lived in Early Spring-and-Autumn Period," *Archaeological Researches* (No.4, 1984), Plate I: No.2; Illustration No.32.
   С.И. РУДЕНКО: "КУЛЬТУРА НАСЕЛЕНИЯ ГОРНОГО АЛТАЯ В СКИФСКОЕ ВРЕМЯ" (Таблица CXVIII), Рис. 129, 130, 131, 132.
8. Gao Zhixi: "A Report of the Result of a Check-up on the Contents of *muguo** Tomb No.3 at Martyrs' Park, Changsha", *Cultural Relics* (No.10, 1959). Illustrations 16, 17.
9. Museum of Jingzhou District: "The Numerous Silk Fabrics of the Warring States Period Unearthed from Tomb No.1 at MaShanzhuanchang, Jiangling, Hubei", *Cultural Relics* (No.10, 1982), Upper and Lower Colour Plates, Plate II: No. 2-4, Plate IV: Lower and Upper Parts. *Jianghan Archaeological Researches* (No.1, 1982), Plate II.
10. *Han Tomb No.1 at Mawangdui, Changsha,* Final Volume (Beijing, Cultural Relics Publishing House, 1973), Colour Plates.
11. Archaeological Research Institute of the Chinese Academy of Social Science: *Report on the Excavation of a Han Tomb at Mancheng,* Volume One (Beijing, Cultural Relics Publishing House, 1980), p.308-311.
12. Xia Nai: *Archaeology and History of Science and Technology* (Beijing, Ke Xue Publishing House, 1979), p.87 and Notes.
13. Two of the more reliable examples are:
    (1) Е. ЛУБО-ЛЕСНИЧЕНКО: "ДРЕВНИЕ КИТАЙСКИЕ ШЁЛКОВЫЕ ТКАНИ И ВЫШИВКИ", 1961, Таблицы II. 6. LIII. М.Р-1207.
    (2) *Han Tomb No.1 at Mawangdui, Changsha,* Final Volume (Cultural Relics Publishing House, 1973), Illustration No.115.
14. Museum of Fujian Province: *Tomb of Huang Sheng of the Southern Song Dynasty Discovered in Fuzhou* (Cultural Relics Publishing House, 1982), p.128-133.
15. Shen Congwen: "On Guangdong Embroidery", *Yangcheng Evening News* (August 9, 1962).
16. *A General Account of the Cultural Relics and Miscellaneous Articles of the Old Capital* (published by the Beijing Branch of the China Travel Service in 1935) has it: "'The Official Nine' and 'embroideries with gold accents' sold by the bag makers in the Qing dynasty were of all kinds and they were famous throughout the country." The "Official Nine" consists of a *dalian* (a long rectangular bag with opening in the middle), a box for containing visiting cards, a spectacle case, a fan case, a watch case, two scent-bags, a thumb-ring box and a tobacco pouch.
17. *The Rule Governing Domestic Conduct of Li Ji* says: "In order to serve his parents, a son . . . must wear on his left side towels, a knife, a whetstone, a small awl, a piece of metal for producing sparks; and he must wear on his right side a piece of jade, a sleeve cover, a sheath, a big awl and a piece of wood for producing fire." "To serve her husband's parents, a woman . . . must wear on her left side towels, a knife, a whetstone, a small awl and a piece of metal to produce fire, and she must carry on her right side needles, keys, thread, a certain quantity of cotton fibre, a bag stitched with needle and thread, a big awl and a piece of wood for produc-

* wooden outer coffin

ing fire." "Youths of both sexes, not old enough to wear hats or hairpins, are required to wash hands and rinse the mouth at the first crow of the cock; then comb their hair and wear scent-bags on their hair knots and the lapels of their robes."

18. *Cultural Relics* (Nos.7 & 8 Combined Issue, 1962), coloured plates on p.3.

19. *Report on the Excavation of an Ancient Tomb with Murals at Yinan*, published by the Board of Cultural Relics of the Ministry of Culture in 1956, Plate No.56 (upper right: a figure wearing at the waist a bag embroidered with a tiger-head).

20. In its part dealing with carriages and dress, the *New History of Tang* says: "In the reign of Emperor Ruizong, knives and whetstones were no longer worn. But military officers above the fifth grade still had to carry on the waist-belt seven articles, namely, a sword, a knife, a whetstone, a needle-case, a flint etc. The readers can find the relevant illustrations in *A Study of the Ancient Chinese Costumes* by Shen Congwen, published by the Commercial Press, Hong Kong in 1981. In Illustration No.96 on page 254 of the said book is shown a Gaochang mural made during the Five Dynasties. It represents Ouigour noblemen with the ornamental waist belt, paying a visit to a temple. Illustrations 74-76 show ladies' costumes of Tang with a waist-belt to match.

21. *Suishangpiao* was a fashionable plaything of the time. It was a snuff-bottle with extremely thin walls carved out of a piece of jade. It was so named because it will not sink when placed on the surface of water. *Zierbenzhi* refers to the thumb-ring made out of pebble-like jade produced in Hetian, Xinjiang. Its price went as high as 800 tales of silver for one piece. Knotting and the use of gold accent were the prevailing skills used in embroidering small ornamental bags.

22. *Report on the Excavation of a Han Tomb at Mancheng,* Volume one (Cultural Relics Publishing House, 1980), p.159; *Han Tomb No.1 at Mawangdui, Changsha,* Final Volume (Cultural Relics Publishing House, 1973), Illustration No.137.

23. Shen Congwen: *the Art of Making Dragon and Phoenix Designs: Brocade Adorned with Gold* (Writers' Publishing House, 1960), p.4.

24. *Suijin* (a collection of gems), a photoprint edition made in 1935 by the Palace Museum, Beijing

Song Yingxing (Ming): *Tiangong Kaiwu* (things made by heaven and hand) (Guangdong People's Publishing House, 1976)

Moe Xiaolu (scriber's notes), a block-print edition published by Juhao Hall of the Wu Family in the fifth year of Longqing of Ming. A photoprinted edition of this was published by the China Book Store in 1959.

Li Dou (Qing): *Reminiscences of Yangzhou* (Zhonghua Book Co.)

Chu Hua: *Mumian Pu* (register of cotton fabrics), one of the series of books entitled the *Historical Anecdotes of Shanghai* published in 1935.

The names of the colours in different shades* which appear in the above-mentioned books are grouped together as follows:

(1) Red and purple - deep red, light red, cardinal red, red of the south, vermilion, cinnabar, persimmon, peach, lotus seed, plum, date, wood red, pale pink, pale rose, pink, crimson, fresh colour, rouge, dark red, pale pink, coral, faded red, Huaian red, never-old-red, *boluo* (name of a plant) red, fallen-leaf-red, pomegrate, apricot pink, *lu*-peach red, real purple, deep purple, rose purple, aubergine, heliotrope, cockscomb.

(2) *Qing***, blue and green - dark blue, reddish blue, golden blue, deep blue, indigo blue, blue-and-green, prime minister's blue***, Buddha-head blue, Gaiyang blue, grape blue, *he*-blue, *tian*-blue (deep blue with a reddish tint), azurite, *fen* (powder) blue, prawn blue, crab blue, egg blue, blue of the first degree, blue of the second degree, blue of the third degree, sapphire blue, greenish blue, sky blue, sea blue, Chaozhou blue, Suining blue, *guyue* (old moon) colour, feather grey, jade white, *yuexiabai* (below-the-moon-white), official green, *guang* green, pea green, bud green, glossy dark green, dark green, willow green, wheat green, lake green (light green), bamboo-stalk green, onion-root green, cypress-branch green, duck-head green, parrot green, grape green, *pingpo* (name of a fruit) green.

(3) Yellow and ochre - golden yellow, bright yellow, cardinal yellow, fresh yellow, gardenia yellow, persimmon yellow, willow yellow, ginger yellow, locust-tree yellow, sunflower yellow, light yellow camel-wool

---

* These names, given by users who lived in different periods of history, were by no means standardized. The same tint might have several names, whose exact meanings are often unintelligible to even professional embroiderers.

** In Chinese, the character *qing* means either "deep blue" or "green".

*** When Cai Jing (Song dynasty) was prime minister, he used to wear blue robes.

colour, reddish yellow, ochre, honey yellow, apricot yellow, corn yellow.

(4) Black and white - black, sweet black, raw black, mature black, glossy inky dark, *buke* black, moon white, grass white, bleached white, ivory white.

(5) Light and deep brown - reddish brown, dark brown, dry ash colour, reddish black, snuff, bronze, chestnut, wool colour, *lu* (reed) dark brown, date dark brown, Jing dark brown, ink dark brown, tea brown, *jie* (straw mat) brown, golden-tea brown, autumn-tea brown, *jiang* (dark brown)-tea brown, green-tea brown, gharu-wood brown, lilac brown, rat brown, musk brown, eagle-back brown, pigeon-neck brown, brick brown, silvery brown, felt brown, camel brown, lotus-root brown, grape brown, onion-white brown, pea-green brown, chaste-tree brown, mugwort brown, frost brown, dew brown, birchleaf-pear brown, oil chestnut brown, sandalwood brown, dry bamboo brown, mountain brown, lake water brown, pearl brown, lotus seed brown.

(6) Gold and silver - gold decoration, *lujin* (gold thread), colours intermingled with gold, *giangjin* (sprinkled with gold), gold edging, *jiejin*, carved gold, twisted gold, sunken gold, bright gold, gold dust, *bangjin*, gold-back, *yingjin* (gold-shadow), *lanjin* (gold barrier), *panjin* (coiling of gold thread), gold knitting, gold thread, fastening of gold foil, *pingjin* thread (gold-wrapped-thread), gold and silver serrated edge, gold and silver background.

25. Deng Yu: "Sichuan's *tiaohua* embroidery", *Decoration* (No.3, 1959).

26. Yan Ming:"Traditional Techniques Used in Making Yunnan Brocade."

27. The purple dye invented by W.H. Perkin in 1856 was at first called aniline purple, later renamed mauveine, and was soon introduced into China. It is the very colour called *yanlianzi* (imported lotus purple) used in Chinese embroidery, noted for its superficial showy effect and a lack of quiet simplicity.

II. PLATES

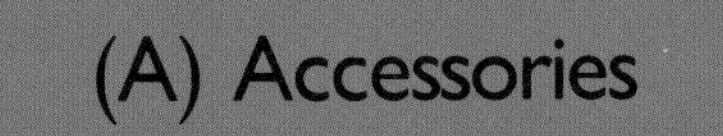
(A) Accessories

1

1. Oval bag worn at the waist with a design of *qilin* (a unicorn) carrying a child. Knot Stitch and Eyebrow Stitch are used, as well as couching with palm fibres. *Qilin* is a legendary animal known for its kind nature. The design is based on an ancient metaphor in which a clever young son is compared to a *qilin*.

2

2. Oval bag worn at the waist with designs symbolizing happiness, wealth and longevity, separately represented by bats, deer and peaches.
The techniques used involve the Knot Stitch and Couching with palm fibres.

3

3. Oval bag worn at the waist with a design of three crabs.
The techniques used include the Knot Stitch and Couching with palm fibres and gold wire. Though the whole picture consists of twenty independent designs, harmony is achieved in the overall structure and tonality. The claws of the crabs are embroidered with threads twisted with peacock feathers (which were widely used in embroidery and weaving in the Qing dynasty).

4

4. Oval bag worn at the waist with the design "From All Corners of the Land".
The methods used include the Knot Stitch, Spreading Stitch, Net Stitch, Scattering Stitch, Close-knit Stitch and Couching with gold wire. The design consists of five gourds, four Chinese flowering crabapples and the characters *shuangxi* (double happiness) and *daji* (good luck), with the implication that everything goes well in the world. Sometimes four couches are embroidered to mean four seas (the world).

5

5. Oval bag worn at the waist, with a tiger design (preserved by Wen Yisha).

6. Aromatic plant bag with designs of plum, orchid, chrysanthemum and bamboo, embroidered with the *Chuosha* (jabbing the fabric) technique. The design, which took shape in the last days of Ming, is otherwise known as "the four gentlemen" and it developed from another design representing the pine, the bamboo and the plum, called "the three friends in winter".

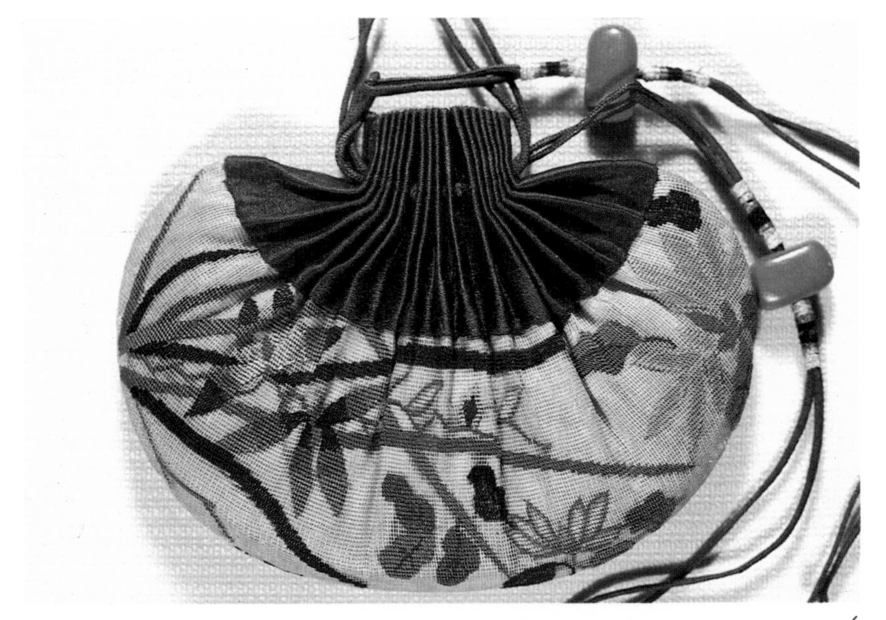

6

7. Aromatic plant bag with flower designs and the character *xi* (happiness) embroidered in Knot Stitch.

7

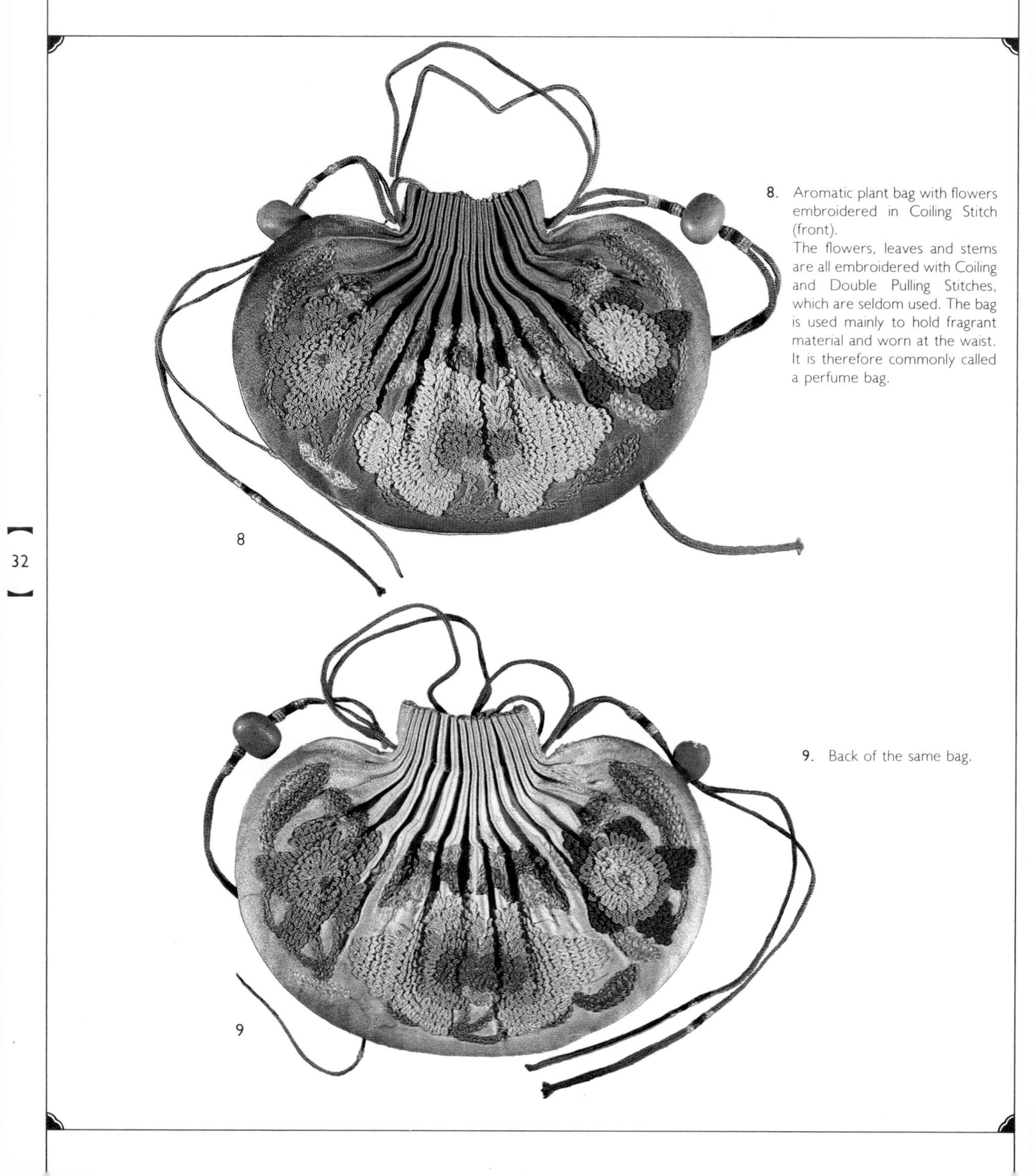

8. Aromatic plant bag with flowers embroidered in Coiling Stitch (front).
The flowers, leaves and stems are all embroidered with Coiling and Double Pulling Stitches, which are seldom used. The bag is used mainly to hold fragrant material and worn at the waist. It is therefore commonly called a perfume bag.

9. Back of the same bag.

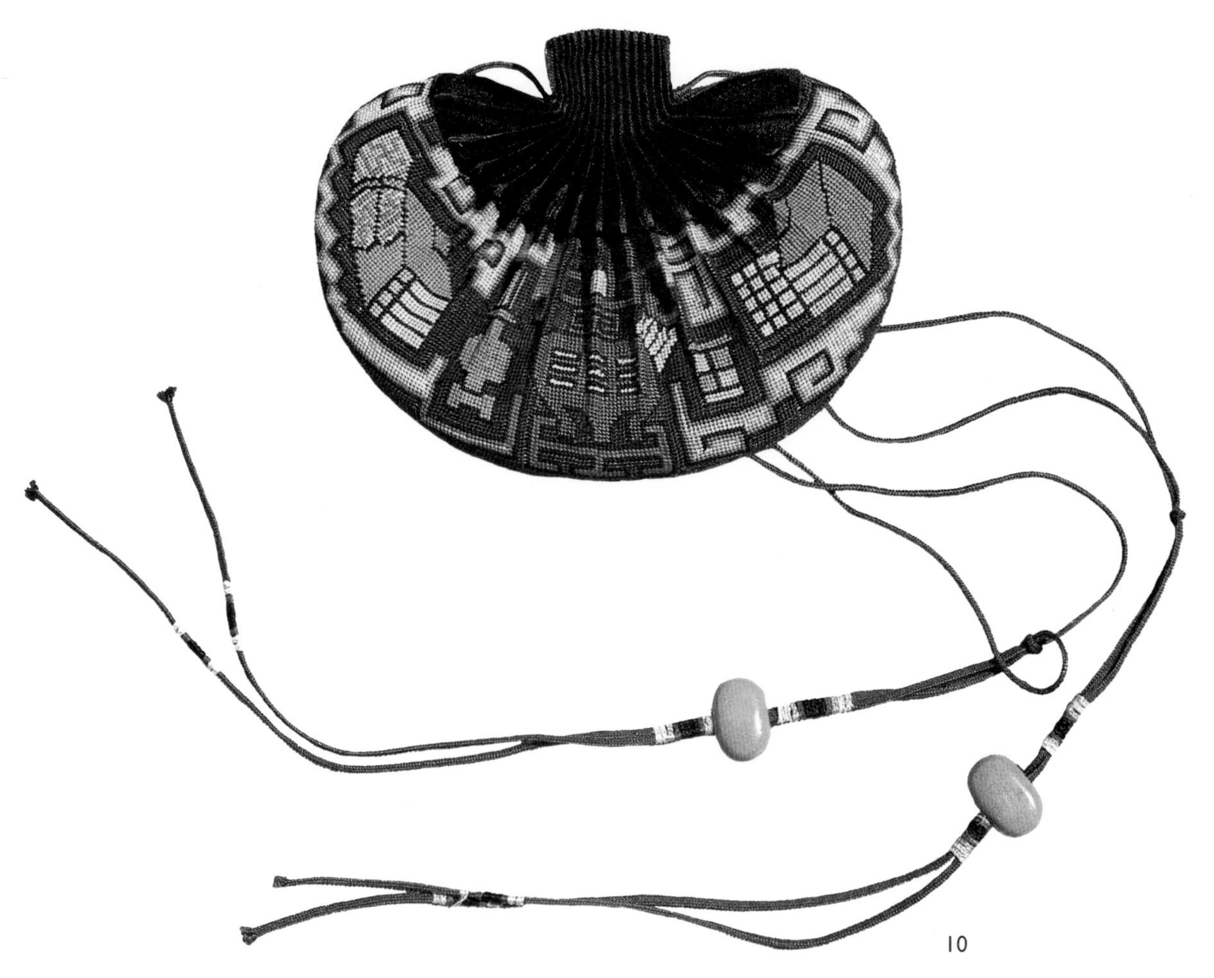

10

10. Aromatic plant bag with a design of ancient objects made by Gauze-embroidering.
The design comes from a Song painting *Xuanhe Picture of Ancient Objects*. It became very popular in early Qing and was widely adopted by painters, potters and weavers.

11

11. Heart-shaped aromatic plant bag with a design of "Two Dragons Playing with a Pearl" formed by gold and silver wire fastened on the ground material (otherwise known as *Panjin* and *Panyin*).
The methods used include Couching with gold and silver wire, Pulling Stitch, and Knot Stitch. The designs are mostly described with gold and silver wire, with the dragons in relief. The metallic wire fastened by colour threads at equal intervals reflects various colours.

12. Heart-shaped aromatic plant bag with deer and cranes (preserved by Li Keyu).
The bag is embroidered with a great variety of techniques. Both the deer and the crane symbolize longevity, and they are puns on two other Chinese characters *liu he*, meaning the universe. The design therefore implies that spring has come to every corner of the world.

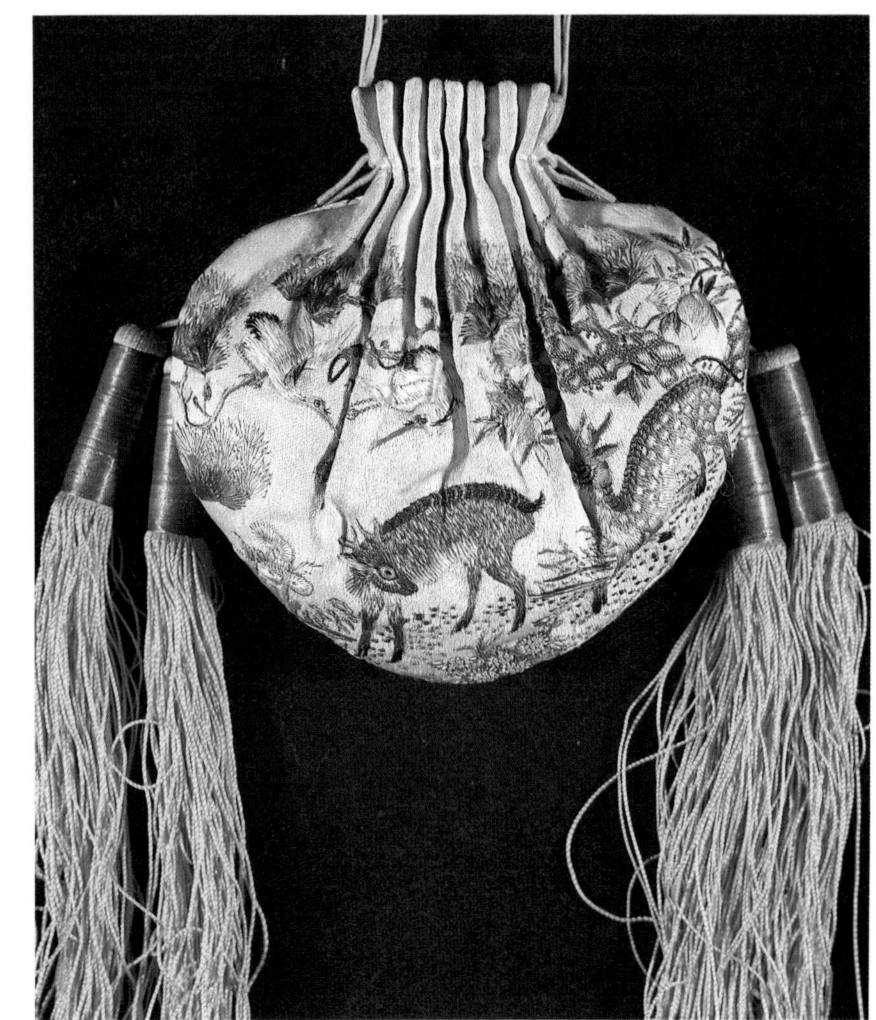

12

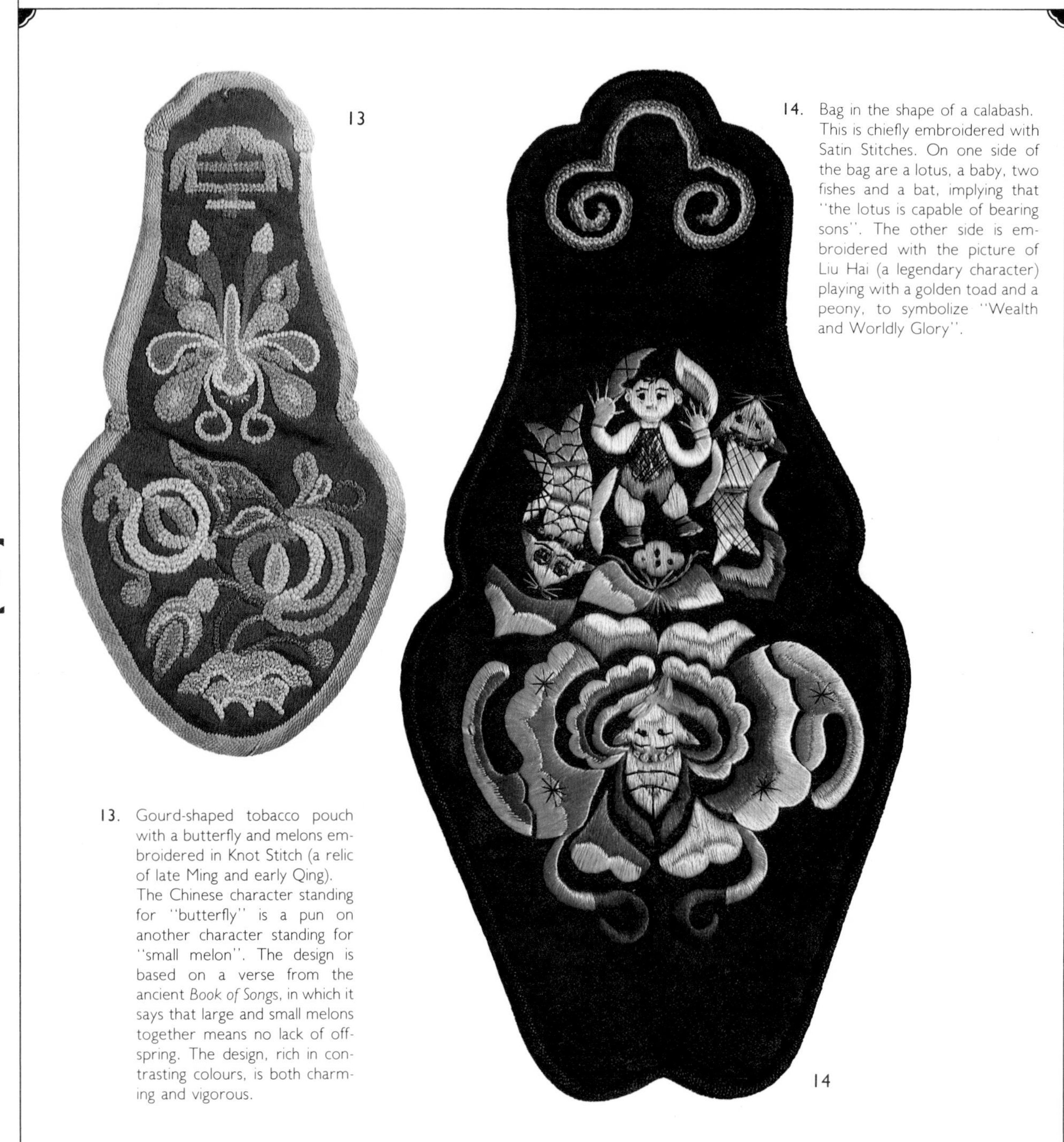

14. Bag in the shape of a calabash. This is chiefly embroidered with Satin Stitches. On one side of the bag are a lotus, a baby, two fishes and a bat, implying that "the lotus is capable of bearing sons". The other side is embroidered with the picture of Liu Hai (a legendary character) playing with a golden toad and a peony, to symbolize "Wealth and Worldly Glory".

13. Gourd-shaped tobacco pouch with a butterfly and melons embroidered in Knot Stitch (a relic of late Ming and early Qing). The Chinese character standing for "butterfly" is a pun on another character standing for "small melon". The design is based on a verse from the ancient *Book of Songs*, in which it says that large and small melons together means no lack of offspring. The design, rich in contrasting colours, is both charming and vigorous.

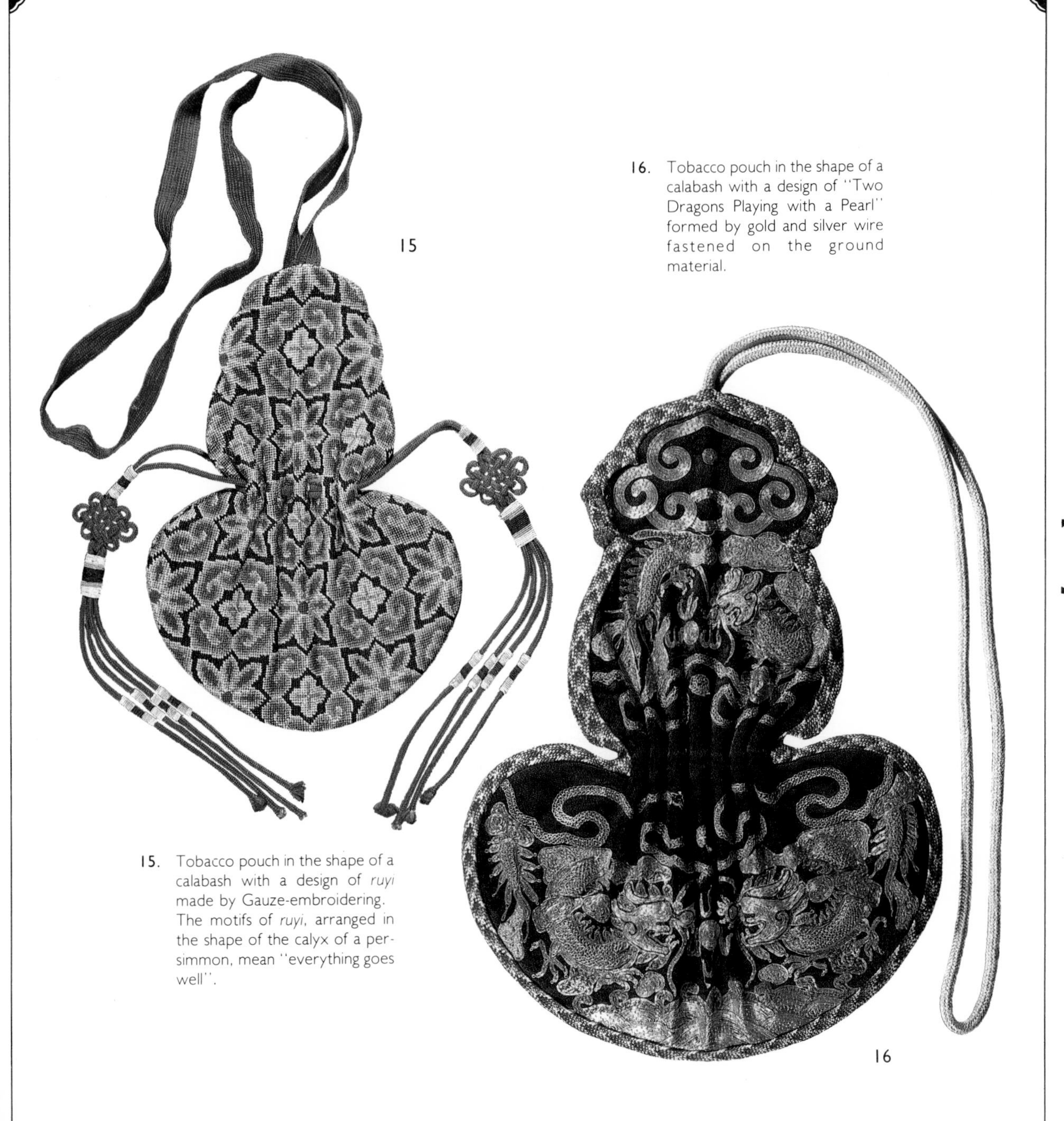

15. Tobacco pouch in the shape of a calabash with a design of *ruyi* made by Gauze-embroidering. The motifs of *ruyi*, arranged in the shape of the calyx of a persimmon, mean "everything goes well".

16. Tobacco pouch in the shape of a calabash with a design of "Two Dragons Playing with a Pearl" formed by gold and silver wire fastened on the ground material.

17

18. *Dalian* with designs symbolizing longevity, made by Gauze-embroidering.

18

17. *Dalian* — a bag sewn up at both ends with an opening in the middle, usually worn round the waist.
It has two patterns,one consisting of two pomegranates, the other of two peaches. Both are made by the *Quan-jin* method (couching with gold wire) and the Winding Stitch, as well as the *Purong* technique. The pomegranates stand for plenty of children'' and the peaches symbolize ''longevity''.

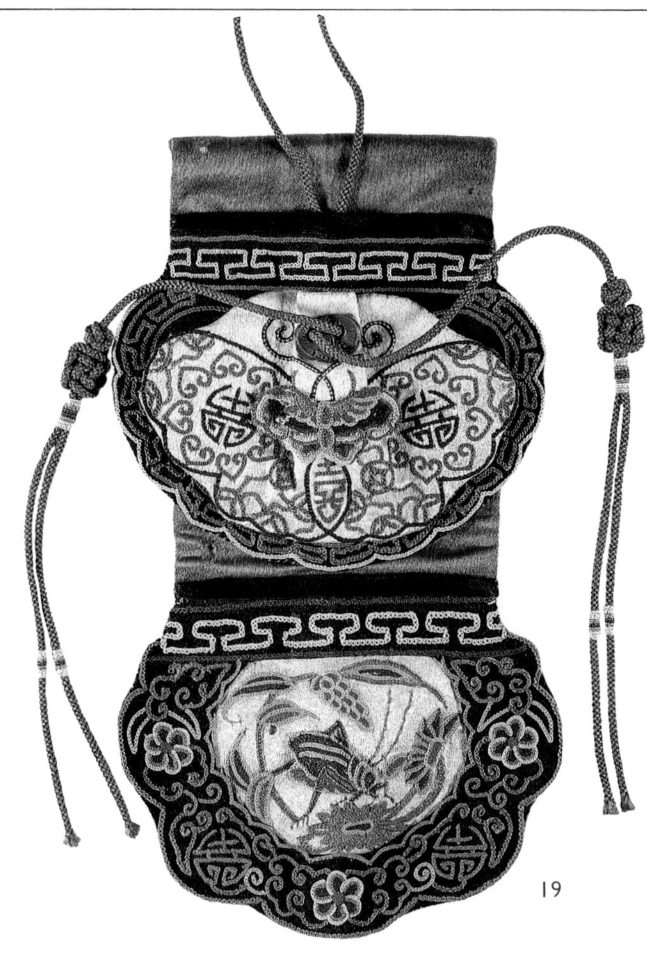

19

20

20. *Dalian* with designs symbolizing "Three Rams Heralding Spring" and "Successful Official Career" (preserved by Li Keyu).
A great variety of methods are used. The three rams symbolize *San Yang Kai Tai*, an ancient Chinese expression based on the *Book of Changes*. This is an auspicious design to show the beginning of a new year with the coming of spring.

19. *Dalian* with designs symbolizing "Happy Meeting" and "Of Benefit to Posterity".
The methods used are the Pulling Stitch and Piling Method. The design in the upper part is embroidered with two butterflies, one on top of the other, with the addition of the characters *shou* (longevity) and *xi* (good luck). Ordinarily, the two butterflies are shown flying towards each other to symbolize a meeting between people. The lower part of the design is embroidered with an insect to mean numerous off spring. This is based on verses from the *Book of Songs* which compare the number of one's children to a multitude of insects.

21

21. Square bag with human figures representing characters in traditional plays, embroidered in Knot Stitch.

22

22. Square bag with human figures representing characters in traditional plays.
The chief methods used are the Knot Stitch, Even Stitch and Couching with palm fibres.

23. Square bag with designs symbolizing "Wealth".
The embroidery is chiefly done in Pulling Stitch, Consecutive Stitch, Knot Stitch, Eyebrow and Eyelash Stitch, Fastening Stitch, and Pine-needle Stitch. The gold-fish, the fish jar and the peonies are all used to symbolize "a hall full of gold and jade" (Wealth), an expression from the famous Taoist writing *Laozi*.

23

24. Square bag with a design of a "Dragon Playing with a Phoenix".
The techniques used are the Knot Stitch, Scattering Stitch, Consecutive Stitch, Piling Method and Couching.

24

25

25. Square bag with melon designs. The methods used are the Knot Stitch, Winding Stitch, Pulling Stitch and Couching.

26. A flat stitchwork, square bag with flower designs in blue.
The chief techniques used are the Layered Short-straight Stitch, Knot Stitch, Winding Stitch and the addition of spangles.
When flowers like the peach, lotus, chrysanthemum, and plum, or when objects representing important festivals like spring festival banners, lamp-rugs, dragon-boats and bags of mint herb (for warding off insects) are embroidered together, the design is called "All the Year Round". It became popular in the Song dynasty and was used to adorn clothes.

26

27

27. Bag with designs symbolizing "Three times top in the Civil Service Examination" and "Entertaining Great Expectations for One's Son".
The stitches used include the Pulling Stitch, Consecutive Stitch, Knot Stitch, Eyebrow and Eyelash Stitch, Pine-needle Stitch and the use of spangles.
Gold-fish and peonies symbolize wealth.

28. Bag embroidered with double threads.
The main stitches used are the Single Close-knit Stitch, Scattering Stitch, Fastening Stitch, Stern Stitch, Winding Stitch and Slanting Satin Stitch.

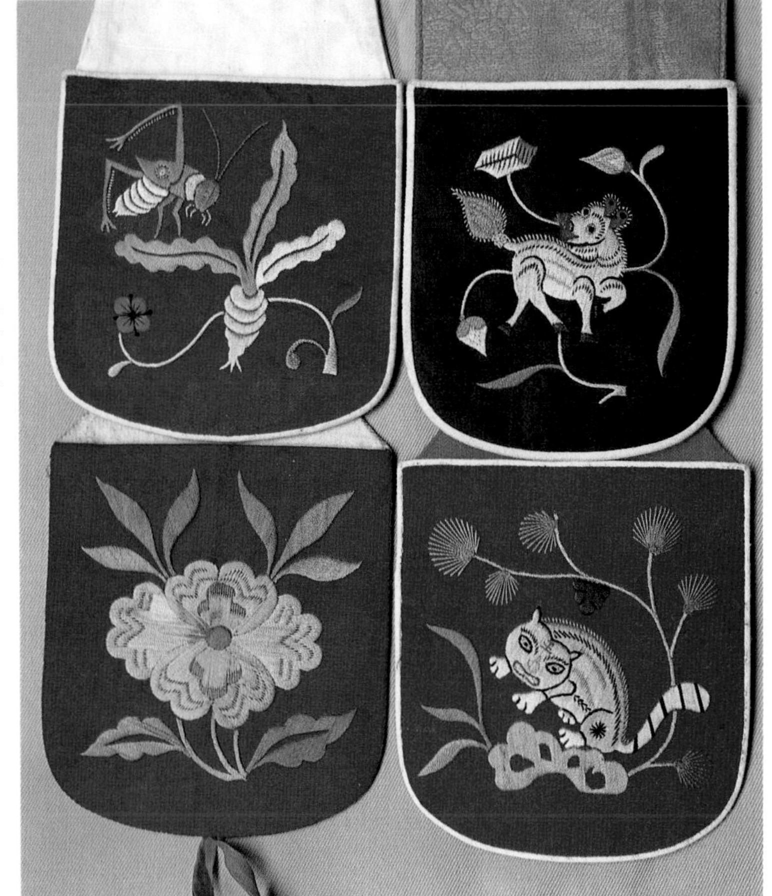

28

29

29. Multicolour-embroidered bag. The chief methods used are the Pulling Stitch, Knot Stitch, Net Stitch and Couching with palm fibres.

30

30. Bag worn across the body embroidered with a lion and eight treasured objects, in coloured threads.
Stitches used include the Pulling Stitch, Net Stitch and Scattering Stitch.

31

31. Bag worn across the body with a design of "Two Phoenixes Playing with a Peony".

32

32. Bag for handkerchiefs, with designs of birds each with a flower in its beak, made by Gauze-embroidering.

33. Bag for handkerchiefs with the design "Two Dragons Competing for a Treasure" formed by palm fibres fastened on the ground material.

34. Bag for handkerchiefs decorated with the Chinese character *shou* (longevity) formed by palm fibres fastened on the ground material.

33

34

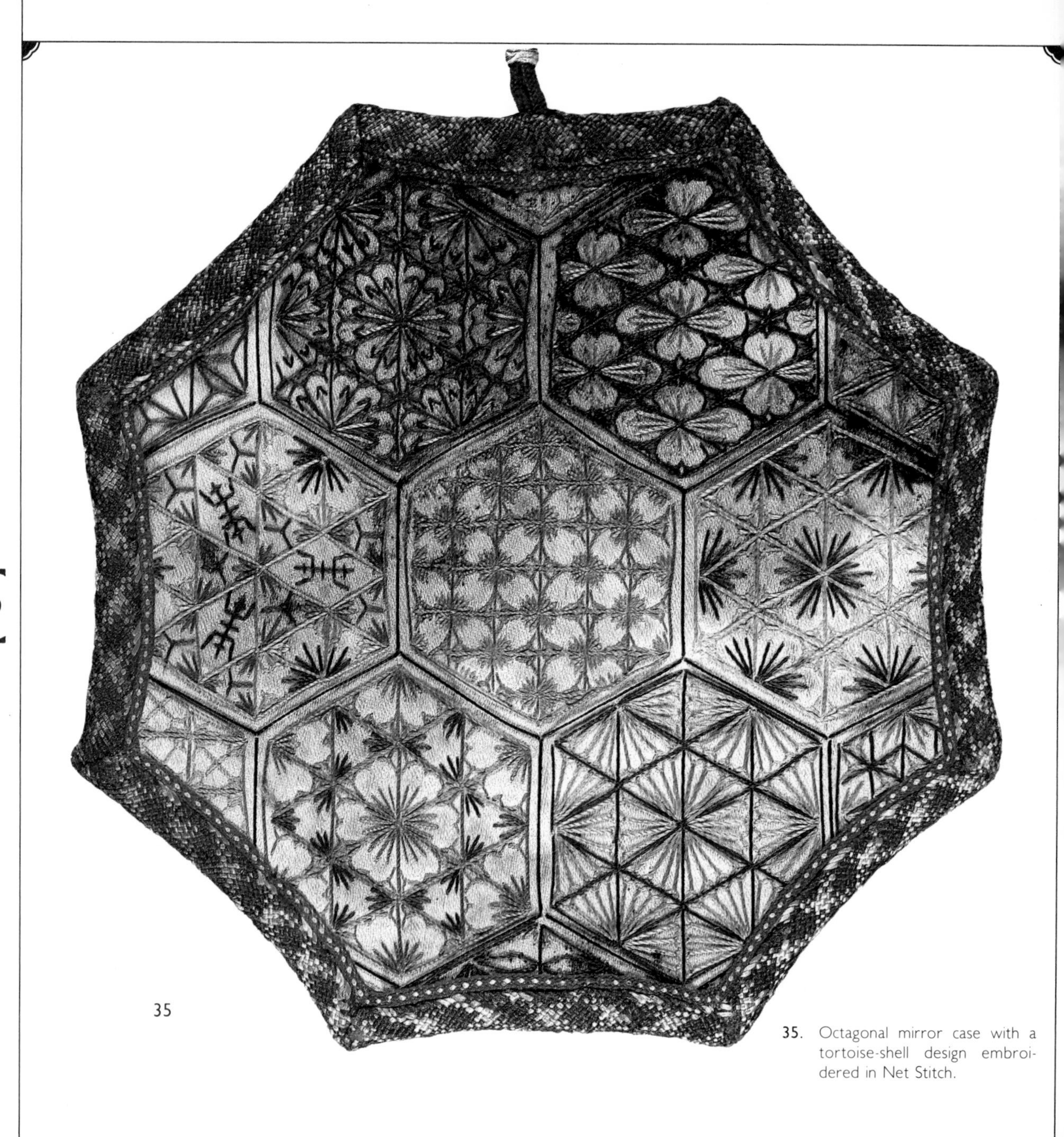

35

35. Octagonal mirror case with a tortoise-shell design embroidered in Net Stitch.

36

36. Round mirror case with human figures and geometric forms. The gauze ground material is lined with gold foil, which shines through its meshes.

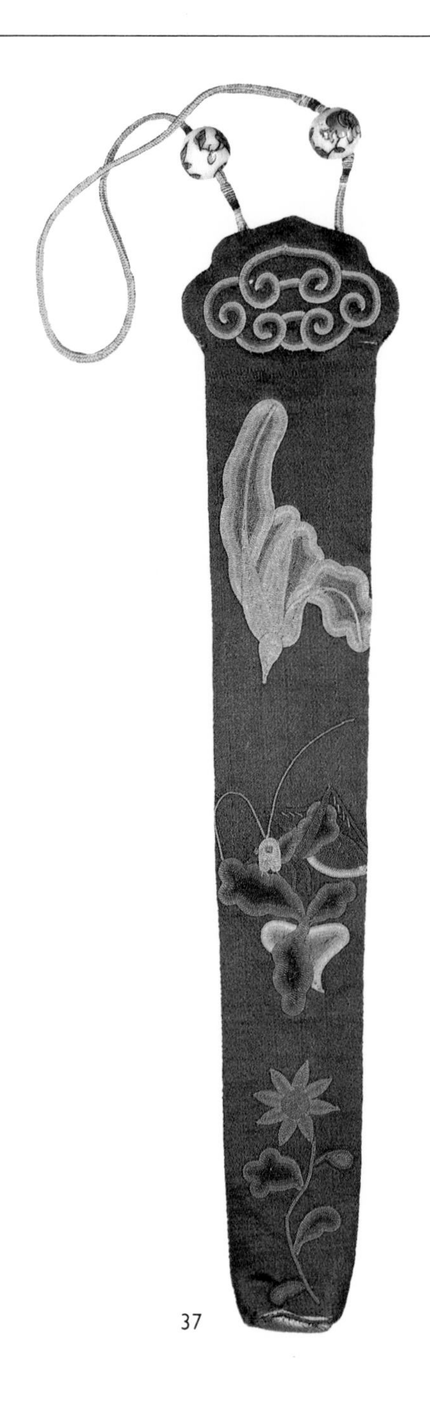

37

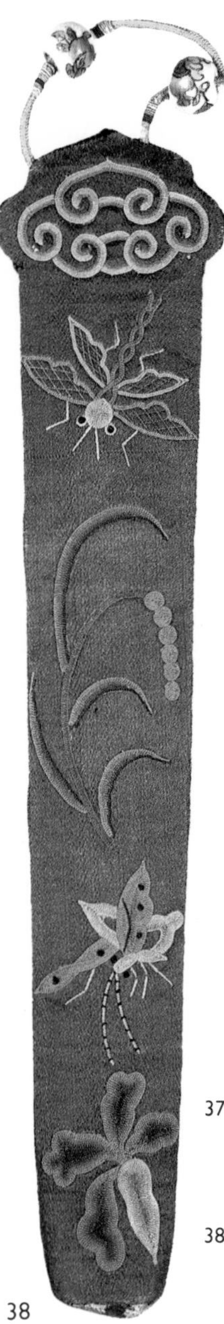

38

37. Fan case with designs of vegetables and insects formed by Couching with palm fibres on the ground material (front).

38. Back of the same case.

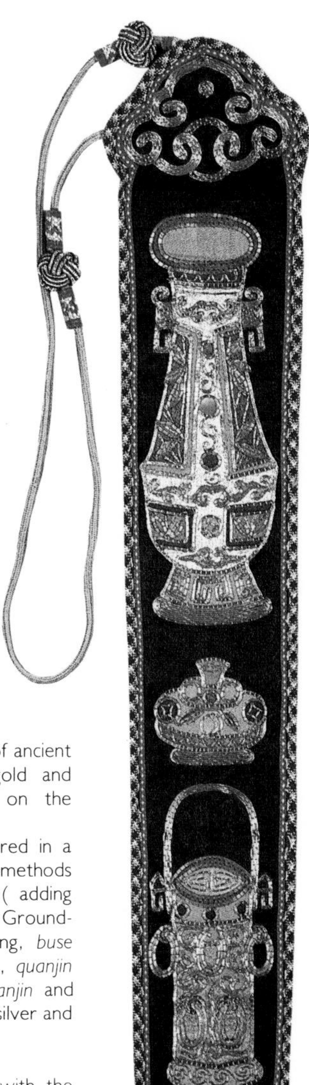

39. Fan case with designs of ancient objects formed by gold and silver wire fastened on the ground material.
This item is embroidered in a unique manner. The methods used involve *Tieling* (adding damask silk cloth), Ground-borrowing Embroidering, *buse* (colour supplementing), *quanjin* (circling with gold), *panjin* and *panyin* (Couching with silver and gold wire).

40. Bag for holding toys with the design "Two Dragons Playing with a Pearl" formed by gold and silver wire fastened on the ground material.

39

40

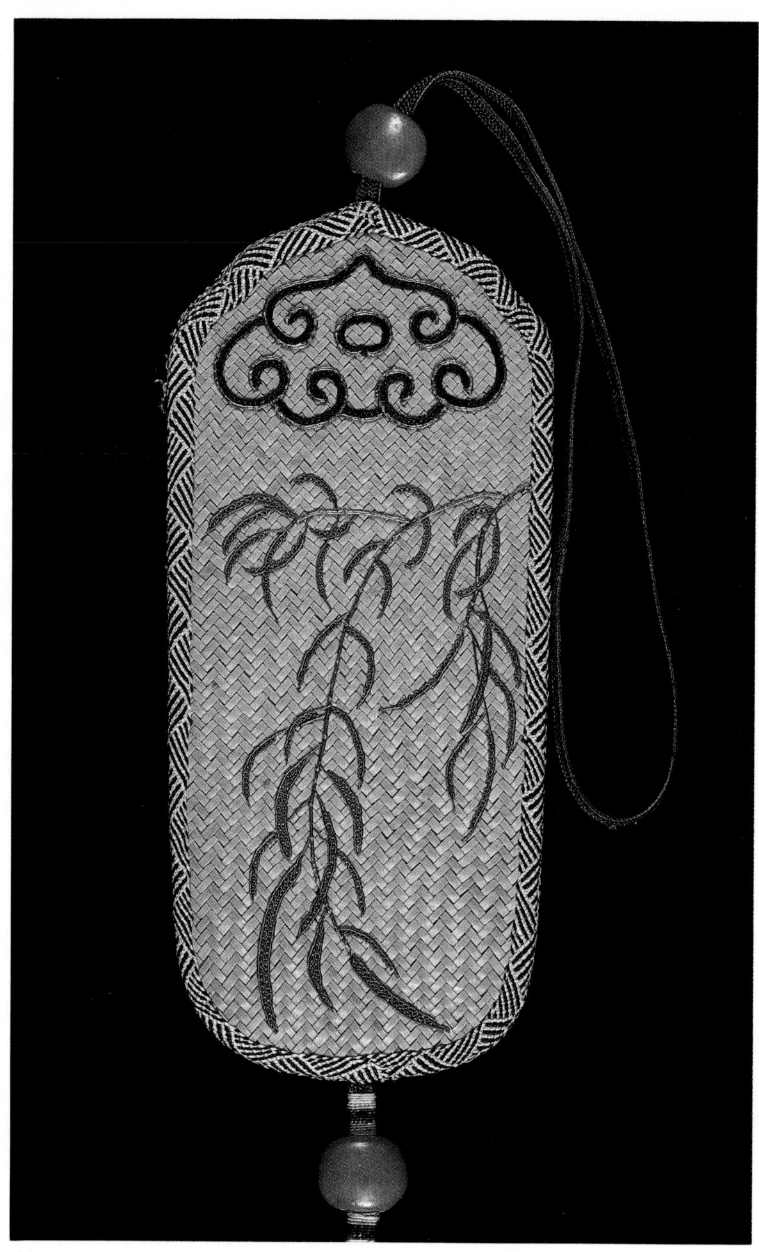

41

41. Spectacle case with the design "Willow Branches on a Mat" embroidered in Pulling Stitch.

42. Spectacle case with a check pattern embroidered in Net Stitch.

42

43. As above.

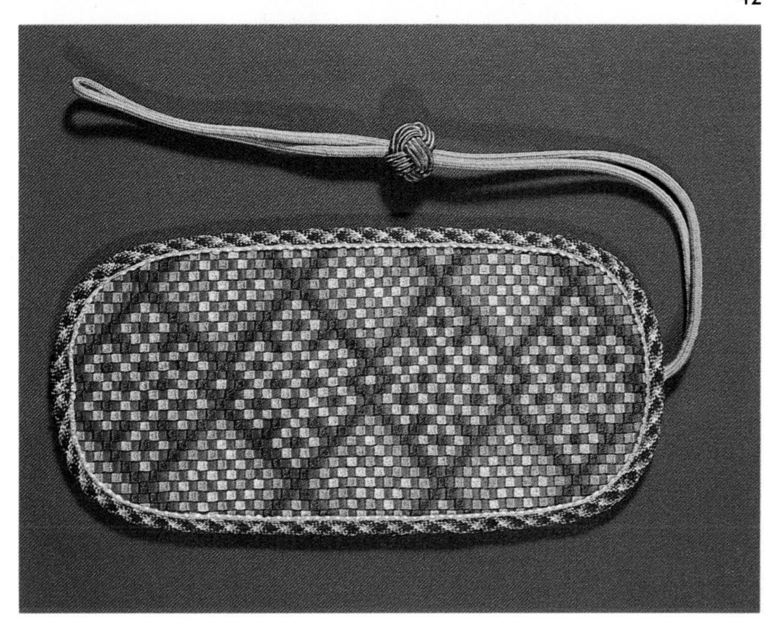

43

44

45

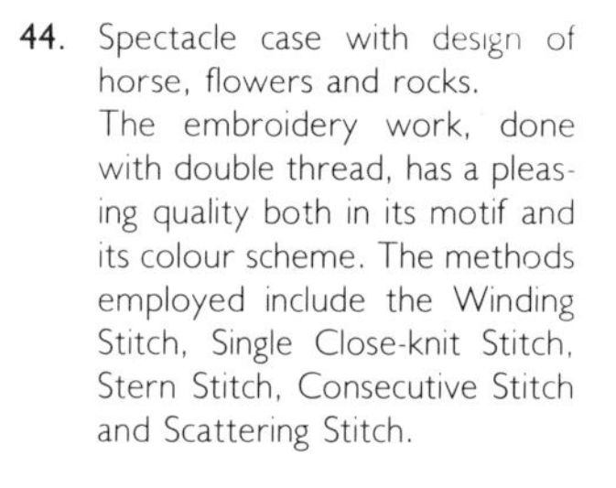

44. Spectacle case with design of horse, flowers and rocks.
The embroidery work, done with double thread, has a pleasing quality both in its motif and its colour scheme. The methods employed include the Winding Stitch, Single Close-knit Stitch, Stern Stitch, Consecutive Stitch and Scattering Stitch.

45. Spectacle case with designs of ancient objects made by Gauze-embroidering.

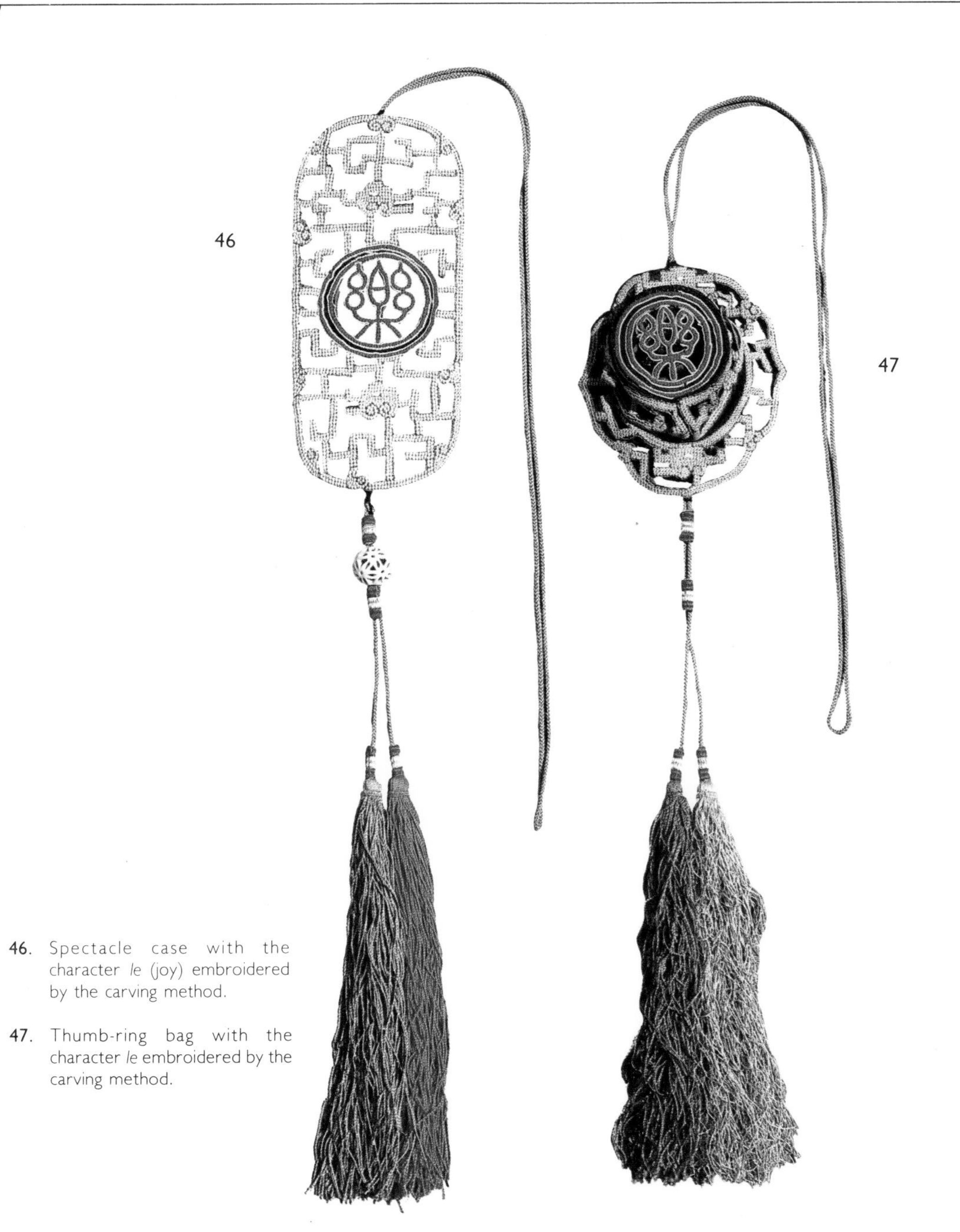

46. Spectacle case with the character *le* (joy) embroidered by the carving method.

47. Thumb-ring bag with the character *le* embroidered by the carving method.

48. Key case with the design "Infinite Happiness" formed by Couching with palm fibres on the ground material.
It is embroidered with bats and seawater to symbolize "Happiness" and "Longevity".

49. Thumb-ring casket decorated with gold and silver wire fastened on the ground material.

48

49

(B) Designs on Clothes

50. Baby's cap decorated by Gold-shadowing Embroidery.
The front is embroidered with a gold calabash. On its left is a design of a "Phoenix Playing with a Peony" and on its right a "Fish Playing with a Lotus". The back is embroidered with the design "Happy Meeting". The edges of the hanging back part are decorated with figures, large and small melons, and the characters *fu* (happiness) and *shou* (longevity). The designs are worked with various techniques on gold foil already cut into different patterns.

51. Part of a baby's cap decorated by Gold-shadowing Embroidery.

52. Baby's cap with the design "Phoenix amid Flowers".
The techniques used include the Layered Short-straight Stitch, Consecutive Stitch and Carving Method.

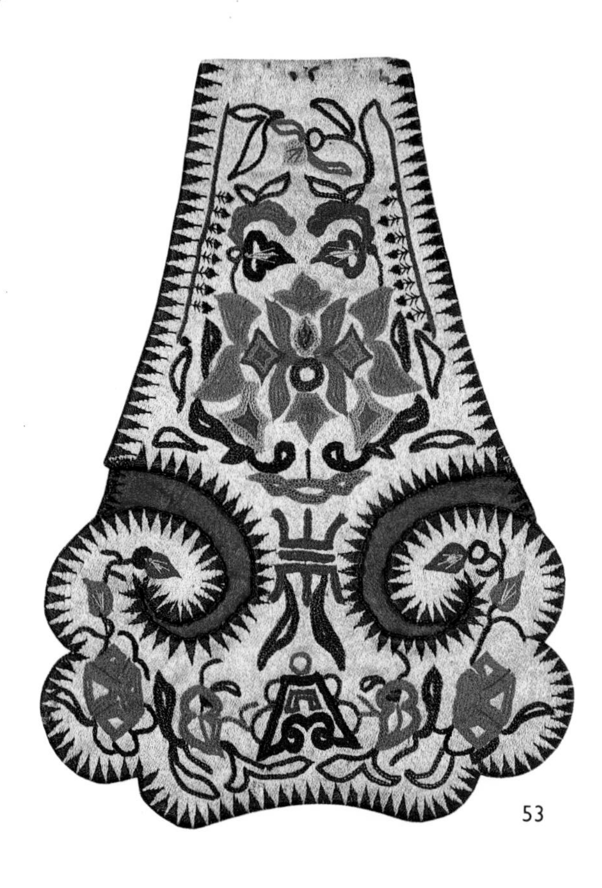

53

54

53. Hanging back part of a baby's cap with an ornamental curve at each side.

54. Hanging back part of a baby's cap with designs of a cat and a butterfly, symbolizing Longevity, Riches and Honour.
The methods used include the Pulling Stitch, Consecutive Stitch, Winding Stitch, Couching and Piling Method.

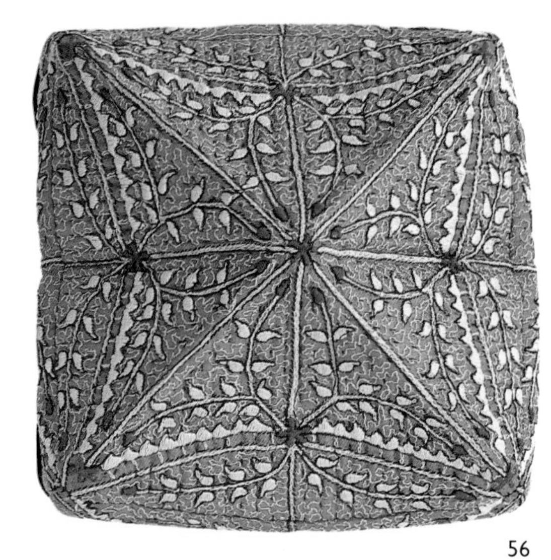

56

55

57

55. Embroidered cap worn by the Uygur people.

56. As above (preserved by Wen Yisha).

57. As 55 (preserved by Wen Yisha).

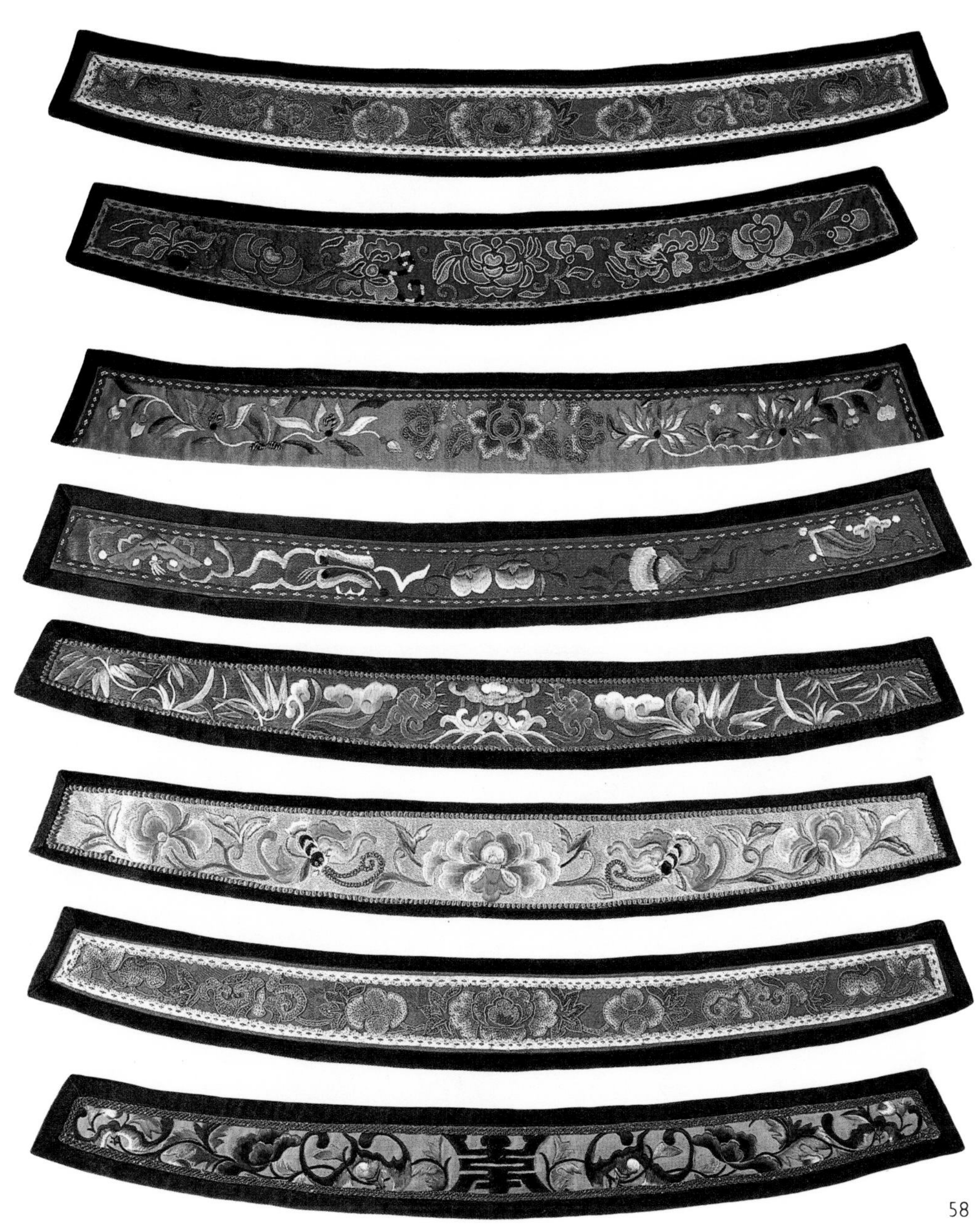

58

58. Multicolour-embroidered collars.

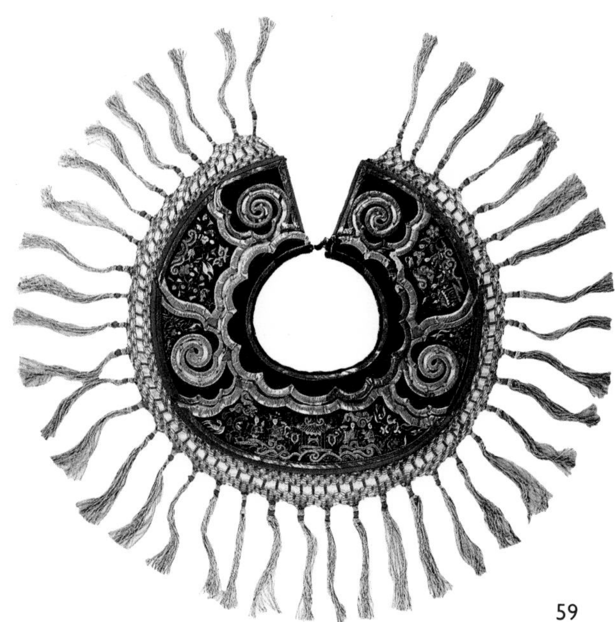

59

59. Gold-decorated collar with ornamental scrolls and a picture representing happy home life. This extremely fine embroidered work is executed with a great variety of skills.

60. Detail of the collar.

60

61. Collar with designs of insects and flowers.
The skills used include the Pulling Stitch, Consecutive Stitch and many others.

62. Collar with a design of *ruyi* (preserved by Li Keyu).
The methods employed include Gauze-embroidering, *Quanjin* technique and Knot Stitch.

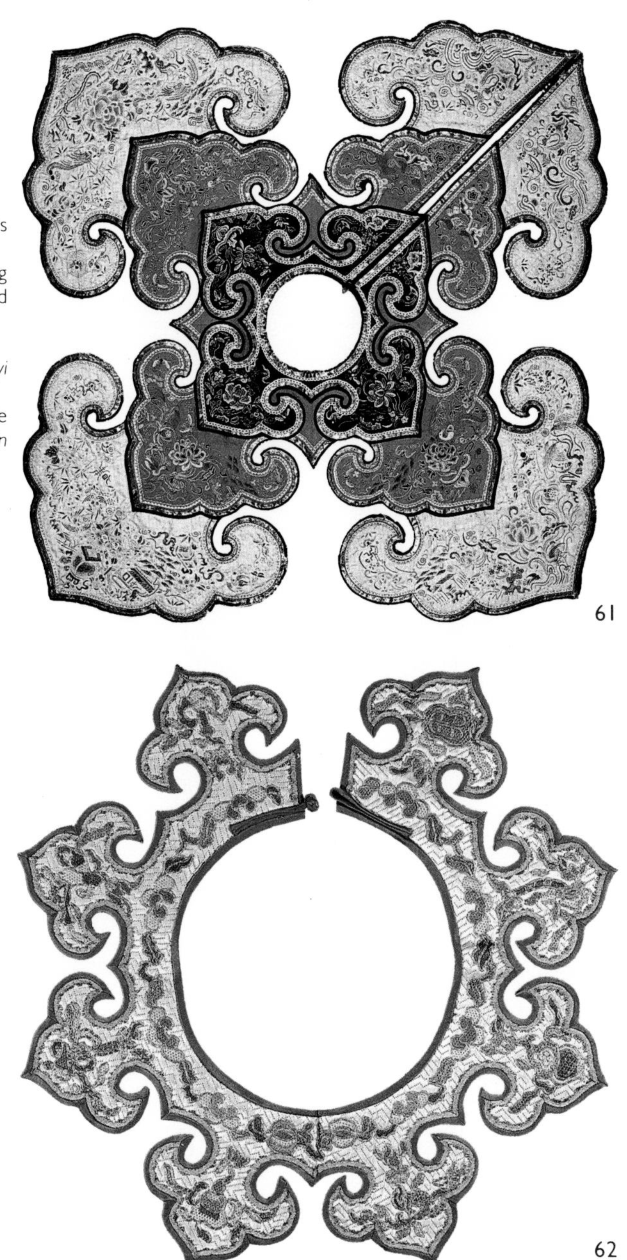

61

62

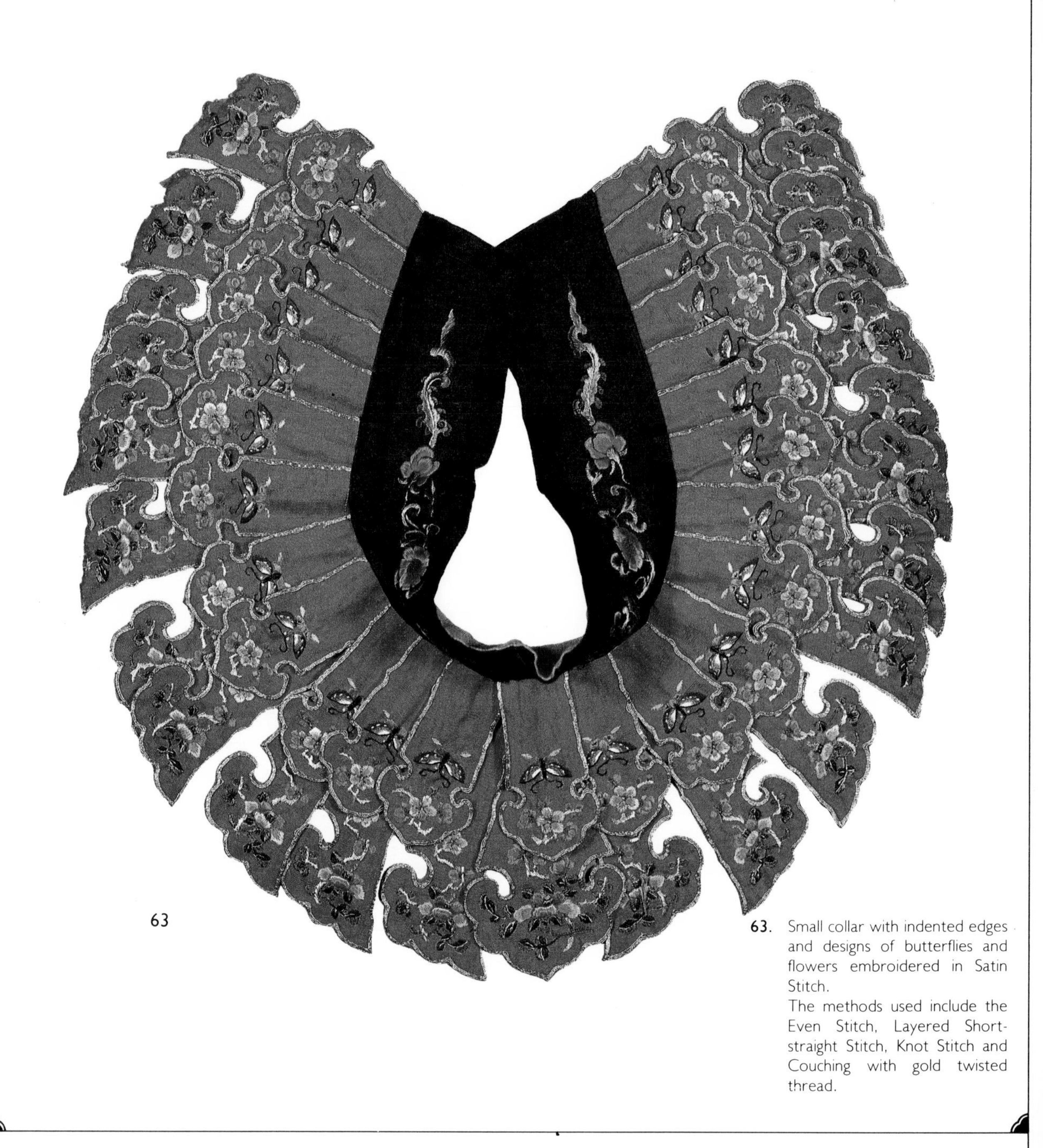

63

63. Small collar with indented edges and designs of butterflies and flowers embroidered in Satin Stitch.
The methods used include the Even Stitch, Layered Short-straight Stitch, Knot Stitch and Couching with gold twisted thread.

64

64. Collar in the shape of *ruyi* with designs of "Two Phoenixes Worshipping the Sun" and "Butterflies Amid Flowers" embroidered in Pulling Stitch. The motif is based on a verse from the *Book of Songs*. It signifies a period of peace and prosperity when the able and virtuous are given full scope and people enjoy happy home lives.

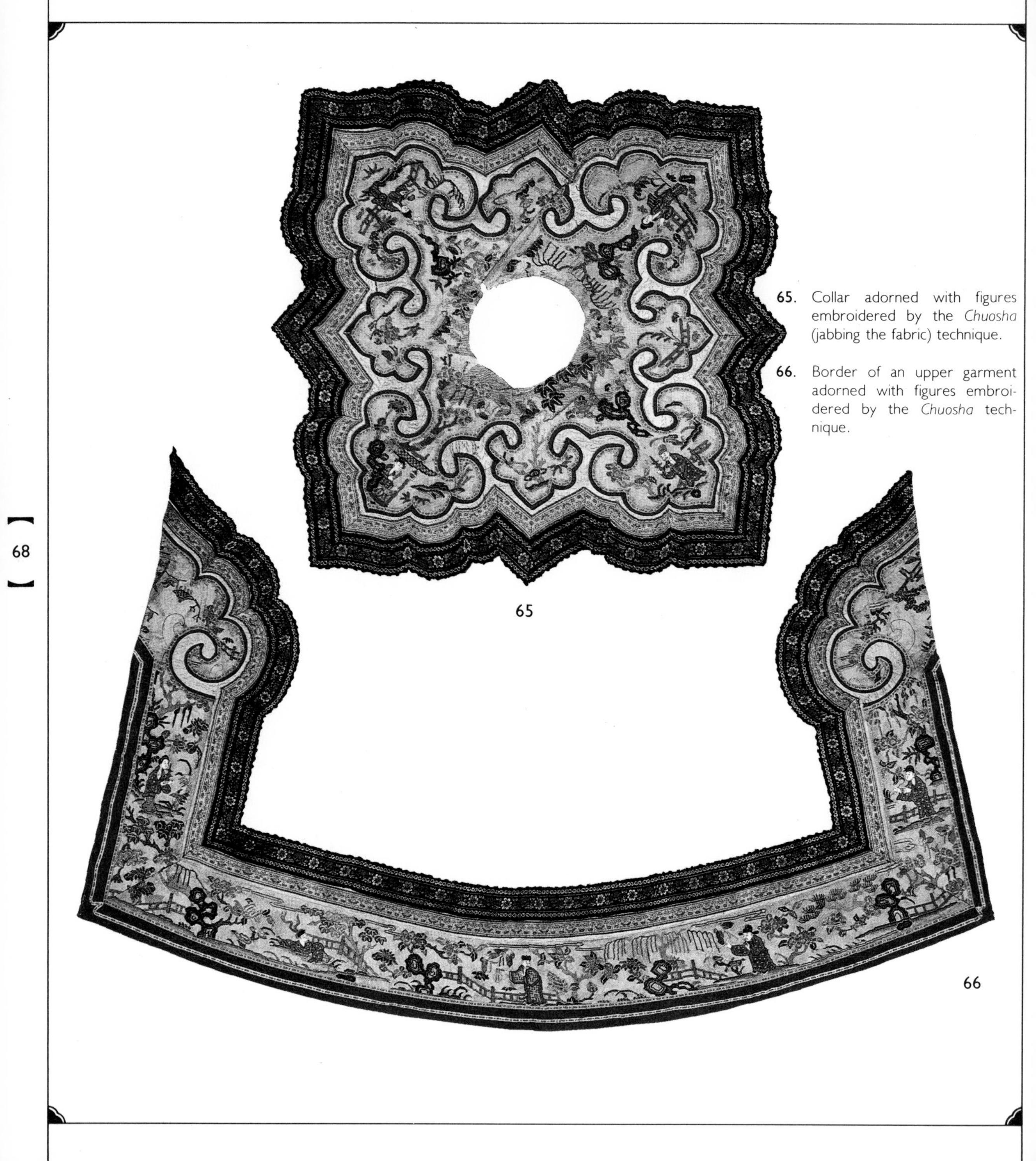

65. Collar adorned with figures embroidered by the *Chuosha* (jabbing the fabric) technique.

66. Border of an upper garment adorned with figures embroidered by the *Chuosha* technique.

65

66

67

67. Part of a collar adorned with figures embroidered by the *Chuosha* technique.

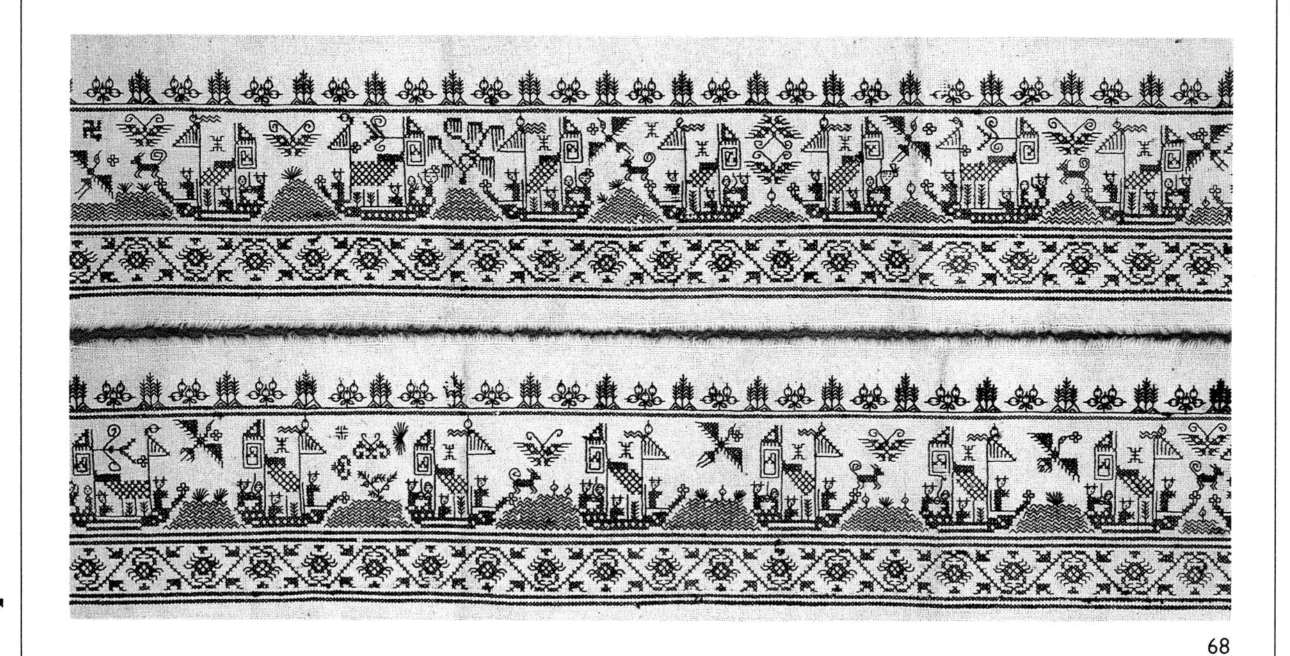

68

69

68. Cuff adorned with designs depicting a dragon-boat race embroidered by the *Tiaohua* (picking patterns) method.

69. Detail of the above.

70. Baby's stomacher decorated with the design "Lotus Capable of Bearing Children".

71. Baby's stomacher with floral designs.

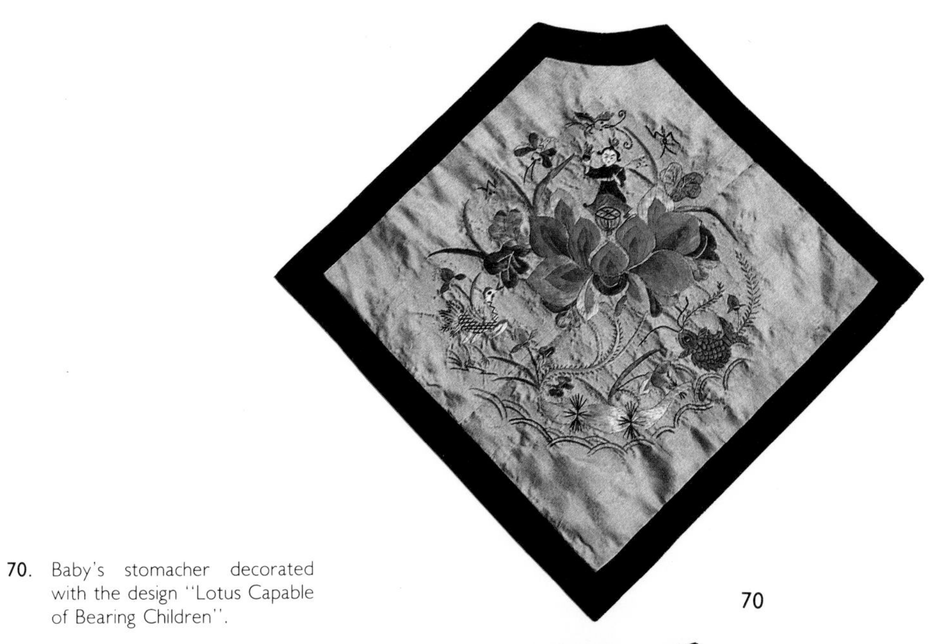

70

71

72. Embroidered wrap.

72

73. Embroidered wrap.

74. As above.

73

74

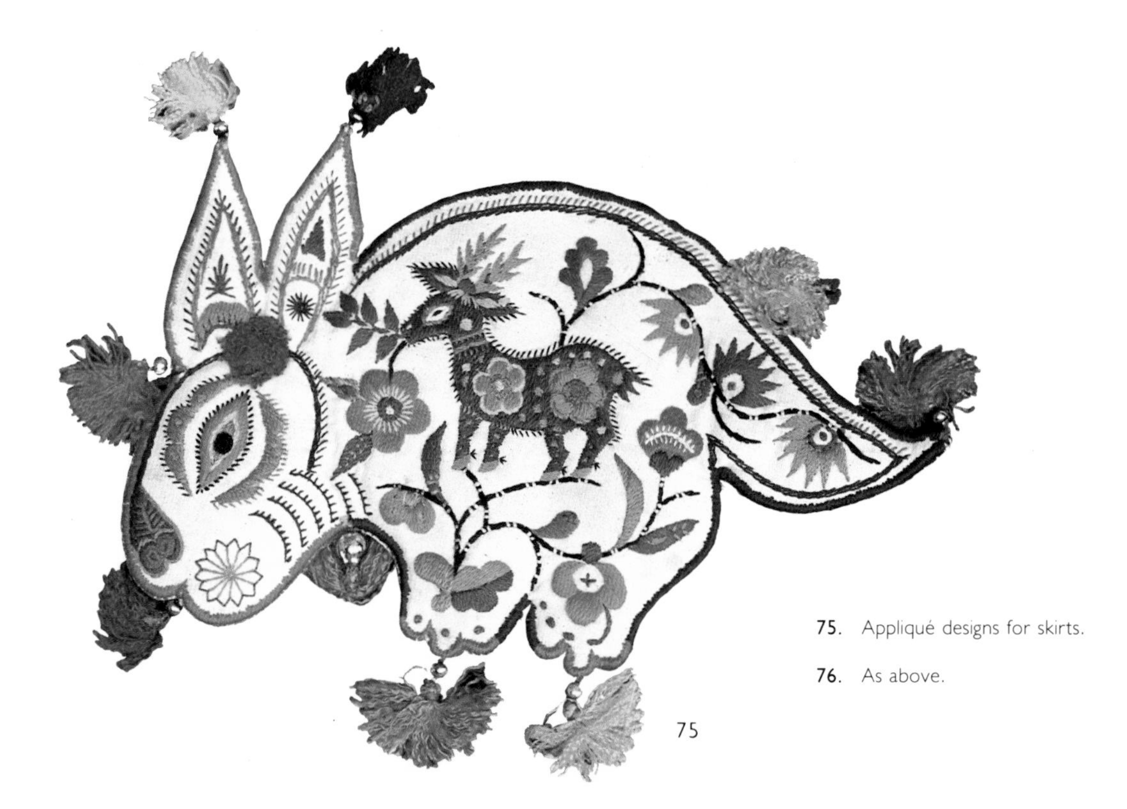

75

76

75. Appliqué designs for skirts.

76. As above.

77. Appliqué designs for skirts.

78. As above.

79

79. Embroidered shawl made by the Hani people in Yunnan

80

80. Detail of the shawl opposite.

81. Shoulder bag made by the Hani people in Yunnan.

82. Detail of the above.

81

82

83

84

83. Shoulder bag made by the Hani people in Yunnan (preserved by Yan Lijuan).

84. Detail of the above.

85

85. Embroidered shoes made by the Mongolian people in Yunnan (preserved by the Yunnan Provincial Museum).

86

86. Shoes with toes in the shape of animals' heads.

87

87. Shoe uppers with designs depicting local life and scenes from folk-tales.
One side of the uppers is embroidered with pictures showing men fishing, cutting-wood, ploughing or reading. The other side has scenes from folk-tales, including "a boy herding a bull", "a bird trying to fill up the sea with tiny stones", "an ox looking at the moon and breathing hard" and a monkey. Some ten techniques are used to make the embroidery.

88. Multicolour-embroidered shoes (preserved by Li Keyu).
The exquisitely embroidered shoes were made by means of the Even Stitch, the *Quanjin* Method, Couching and Knot Stitch.

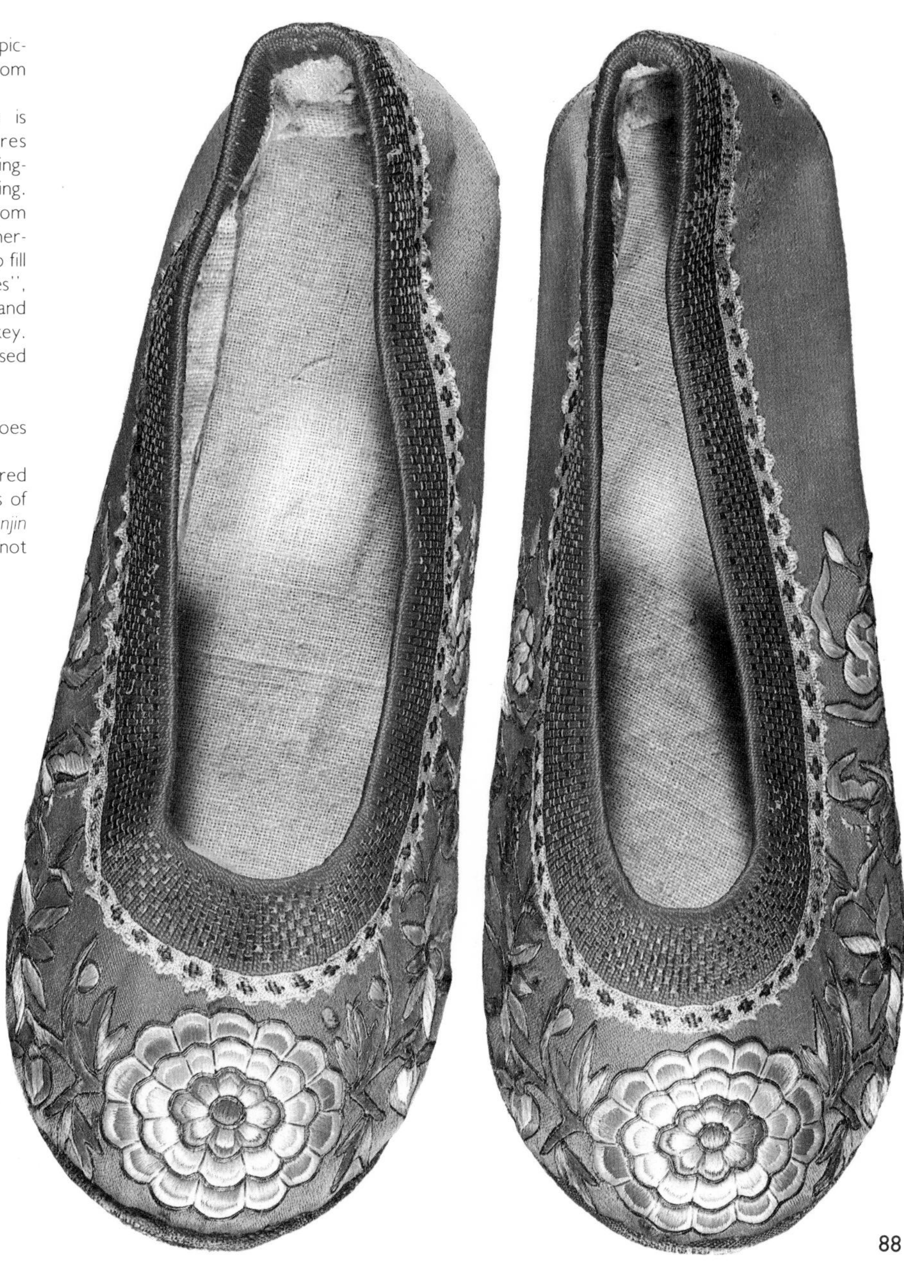
88

89

89. Puttees worn by women (preserved by Li Keyu).
Stitches used include the Even Stitch, Fastening Stitch, and *Quanjin* Method.

(C) Embroidered Household Articles

90

91

90. Door curtain made in Chaoyang, Liaoning.

91. Detail of the above.

92. Detail of 90.

93. Detail of 90.

92

93

94

94. Door-curtain embroidered by the *Tiaohua* (picking patterns) method, by the Miao people in Hunan (preserved by Shen Congwen).

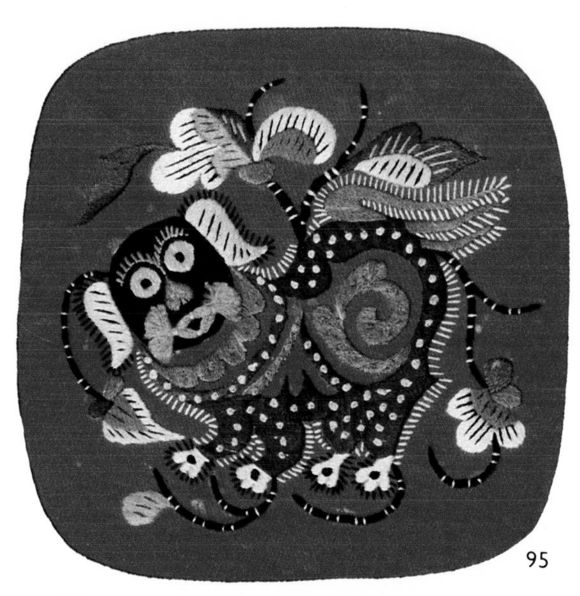

95. Pillow slip.

96. Pillow slip.

97. Pillow slip.

98. Pillow slip.

99. Pillow slip with a rat design, made in Guangyuan, Sichuan.

100. Pillow slip with a phoenix design, made in Guangyuan, Sichuan.

99

100

101

101. Pillow slip.

102. Pillow slip.

103. Pillow slip.

102

103

104

105

104. Decoration on top of hexagonal box for holding needles and thread made in Chaoyang, Liaoning.

105. Side view of the same box.

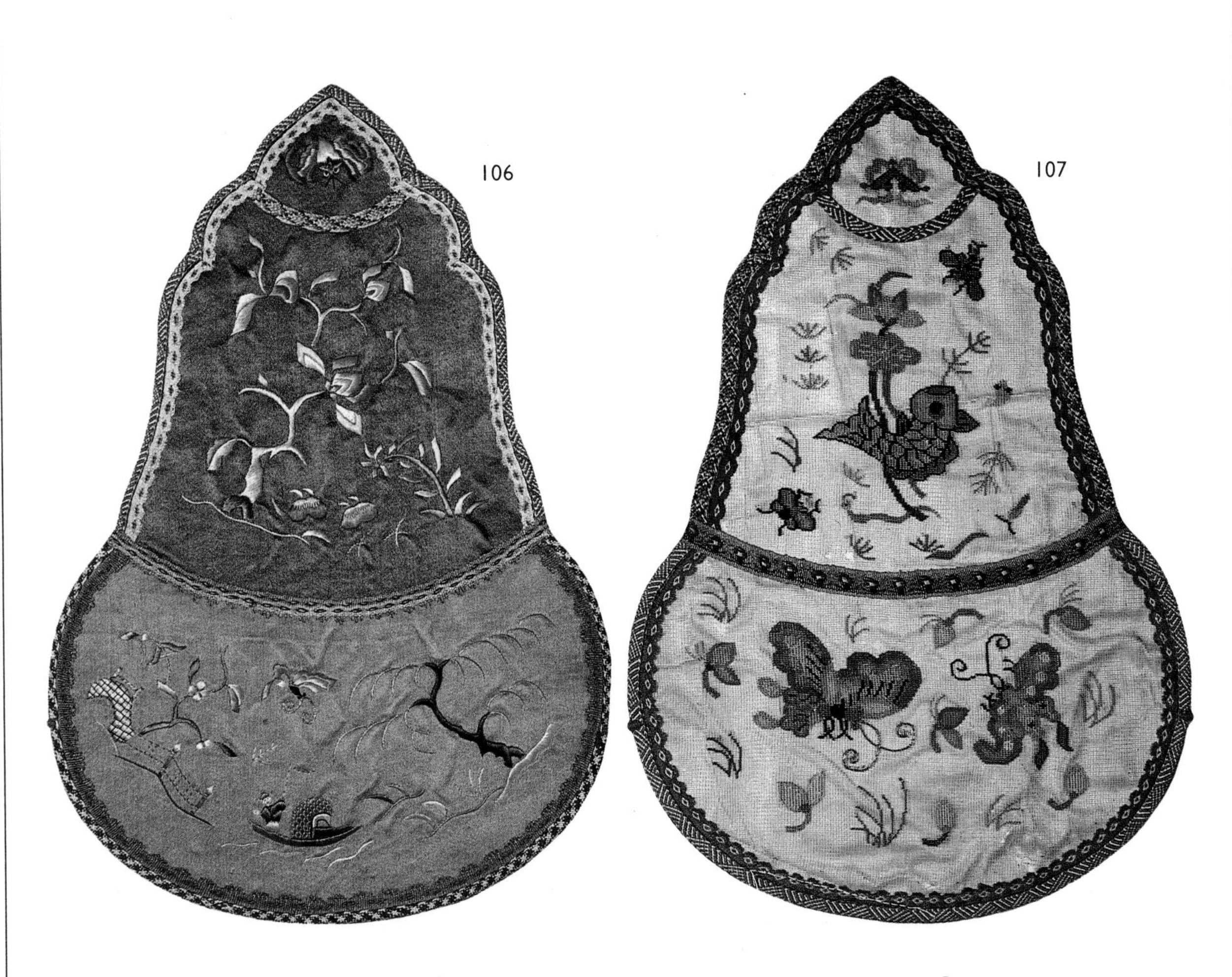

106. Scissors case, preserved by the Central Arts and Crafts Academy.

107. Scissors case made by Gauze-embroidering.

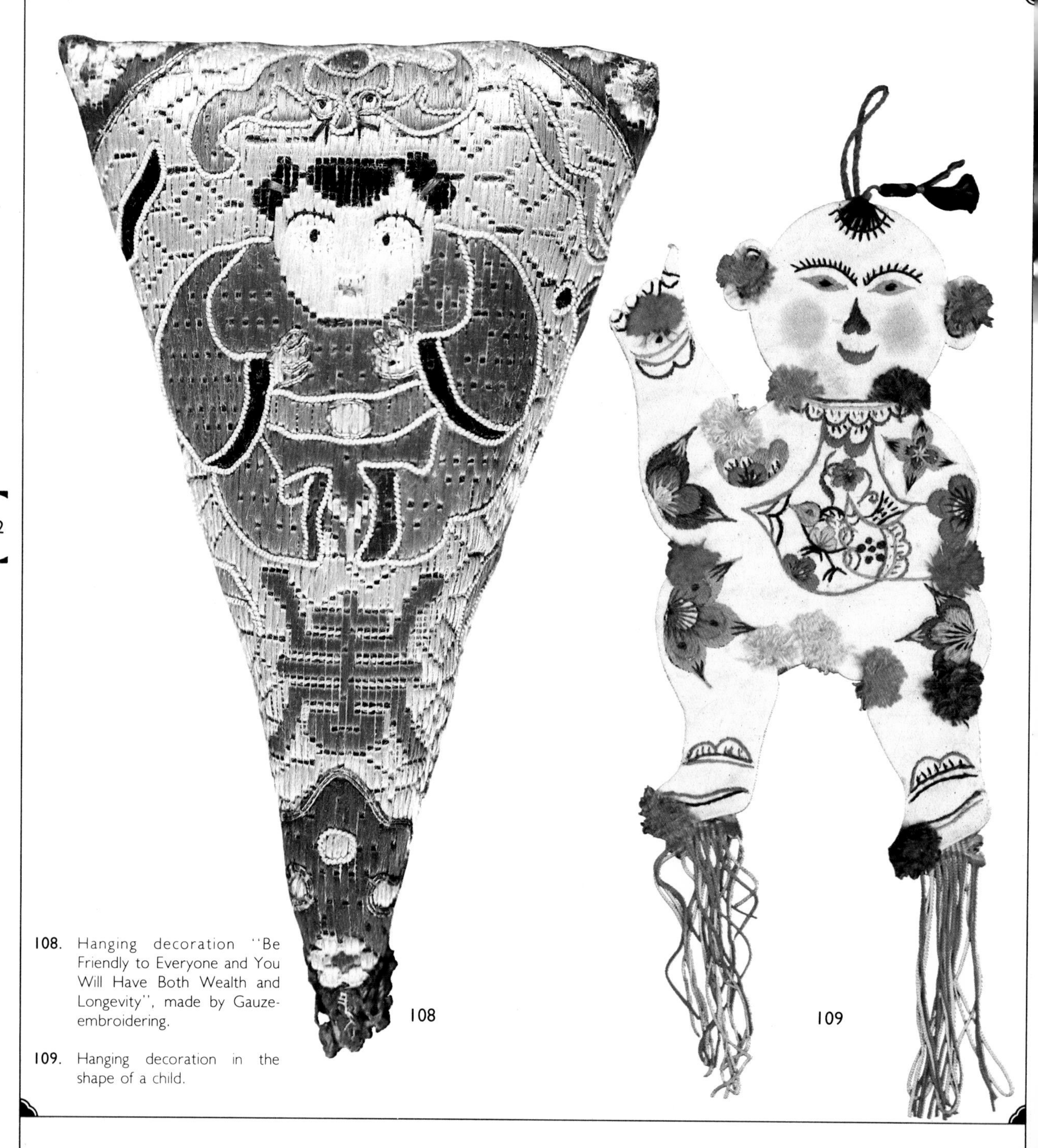

108. Hanging decoration "Be Friendly to Everyone and You Will Have Both Wealth and Longevity", made by Gauze-embroidering.

109. Hanging decoration in the shape of a child.

110

110. Hanging decoration in the shape of a fan made by Gauze-embroidering (preserved by Wen Yisha).

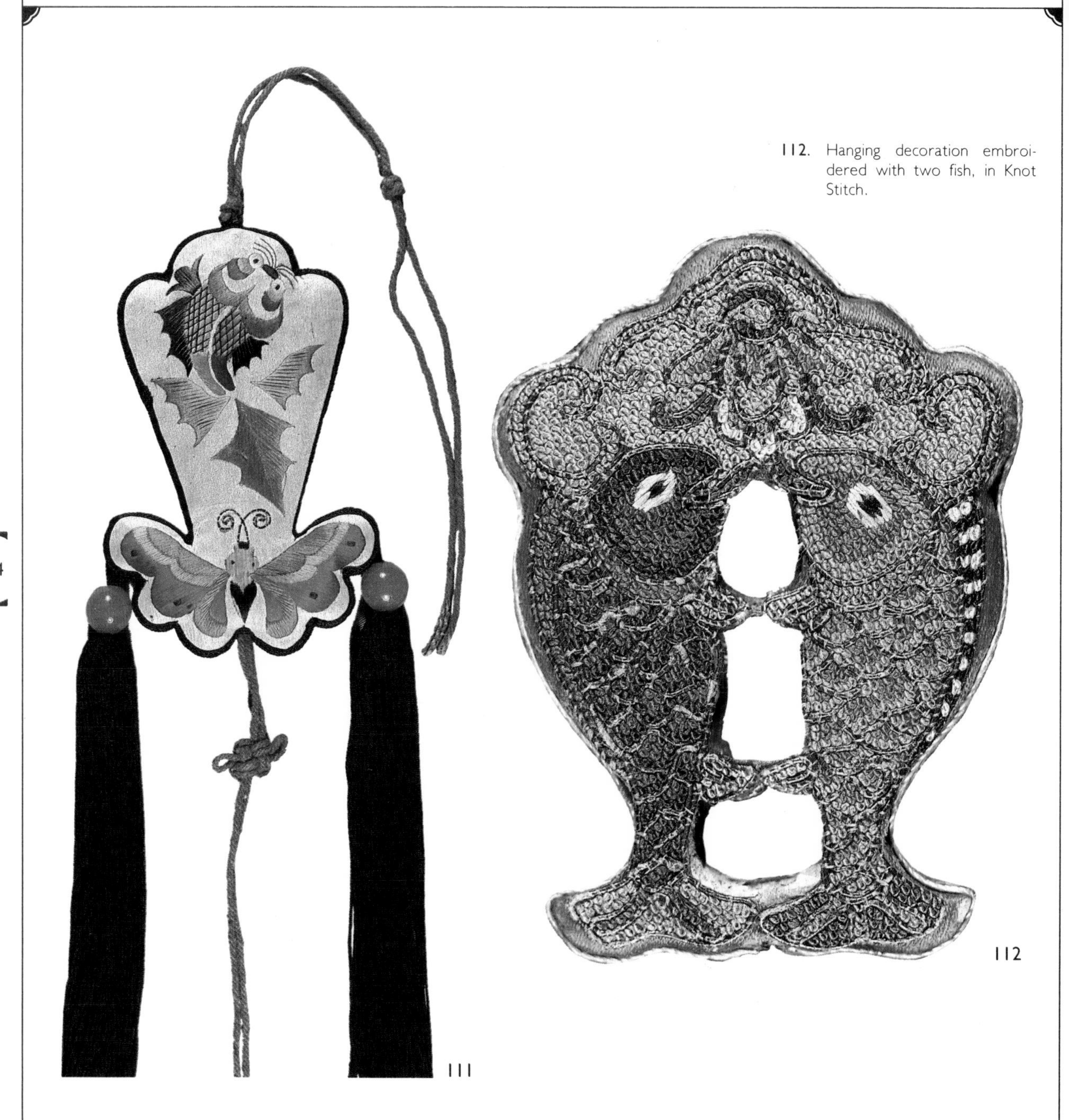

112. Hanging decoration embroidered with two fish, in Knot Stitch.

111. Hanging decoration.

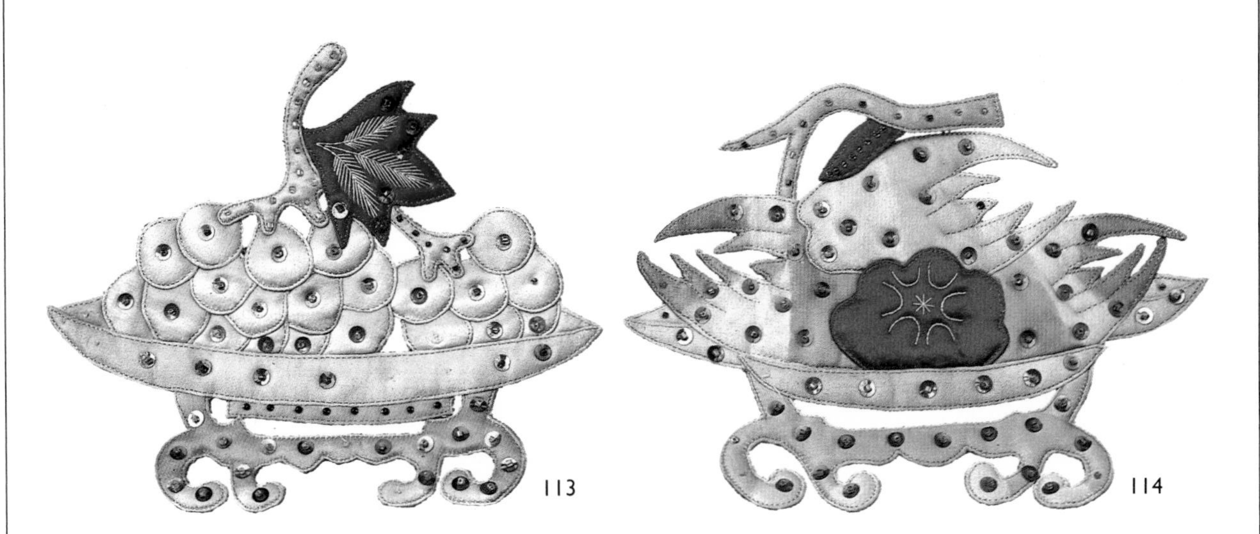

113. Hanging decoration embroidered by the *baohua* method.

114. Back view of the above.

115. Gold-edged hanging decoration with two decorative curves in the middle and designs embroidered in Knot Stitch.

116. Hanging decoration embroidered by the *baohua* technique and adorned with pearls.

116

D) Designs In Chinese Embroidery

117-123 Dragon Designs

117

118

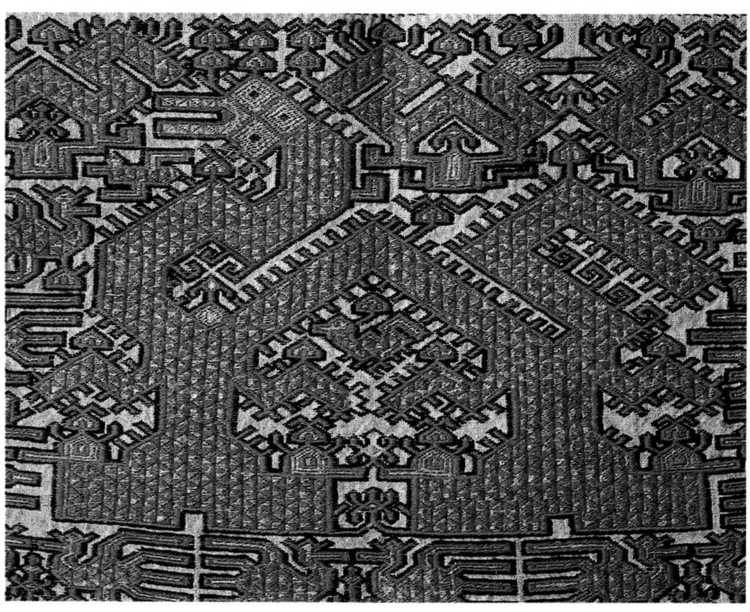

119

120

121

122

123

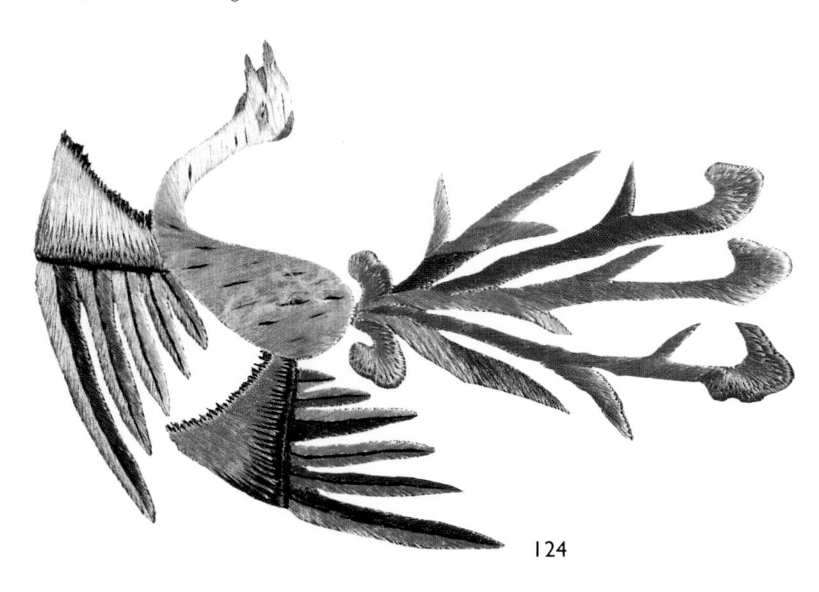

124

125

126

127

128

129

130

131

132

133

134

135

136

137

137-150 Bird Designs

138

139

140

141

142

143

144

145

146

147

148

149

150

151

152

153

154

155

156

157

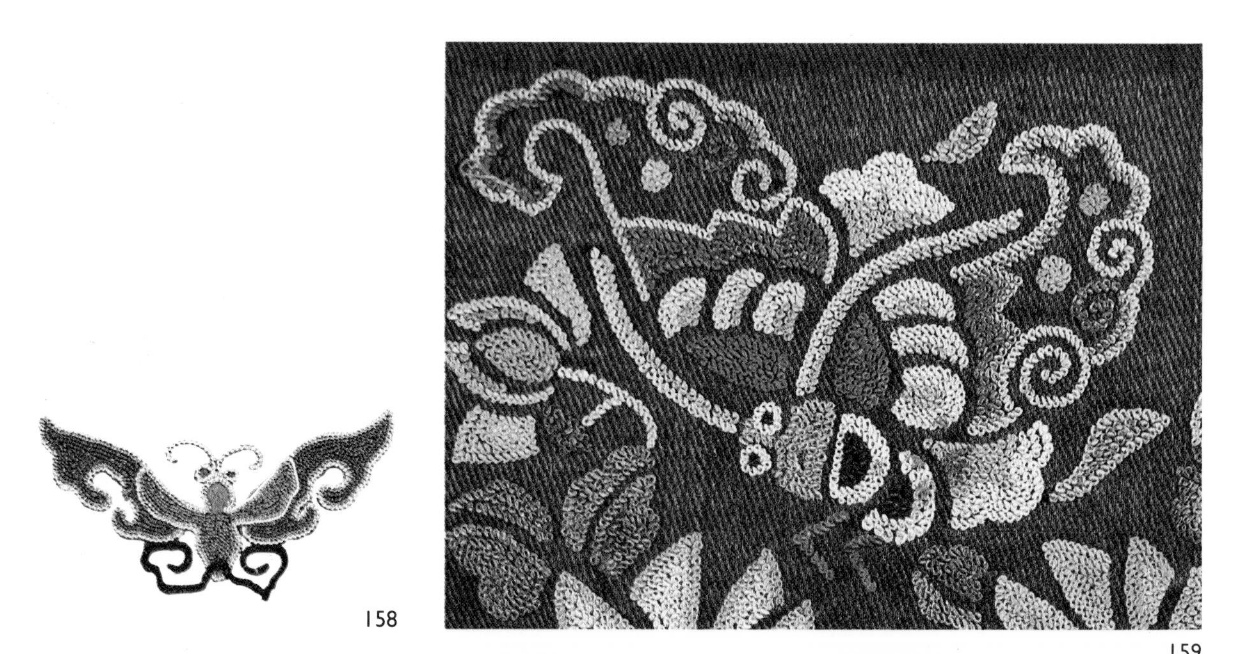

158

159

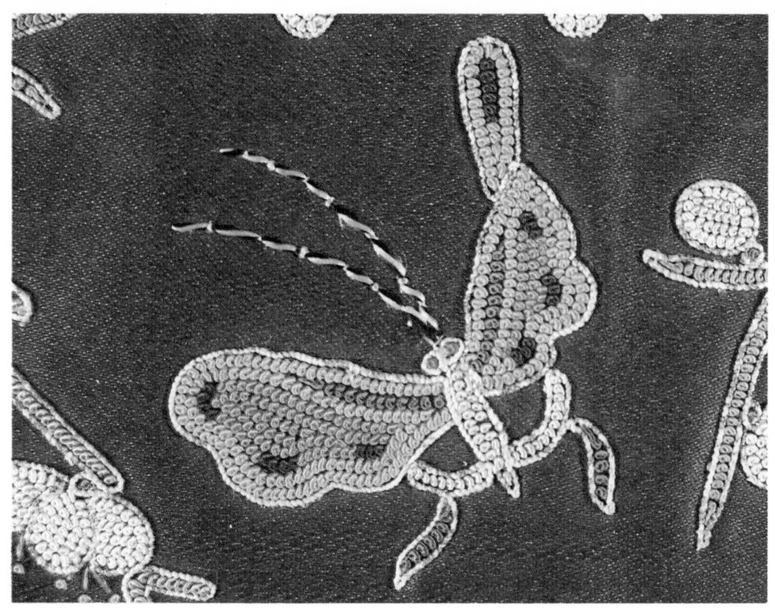

160

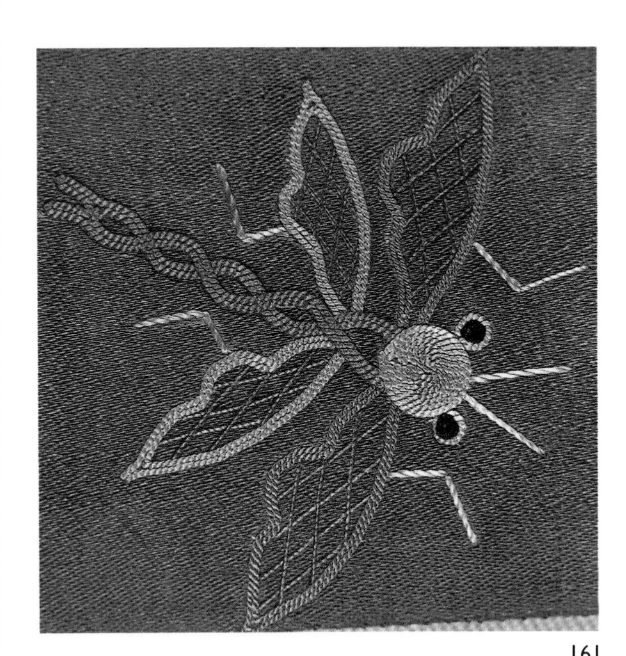

161

162

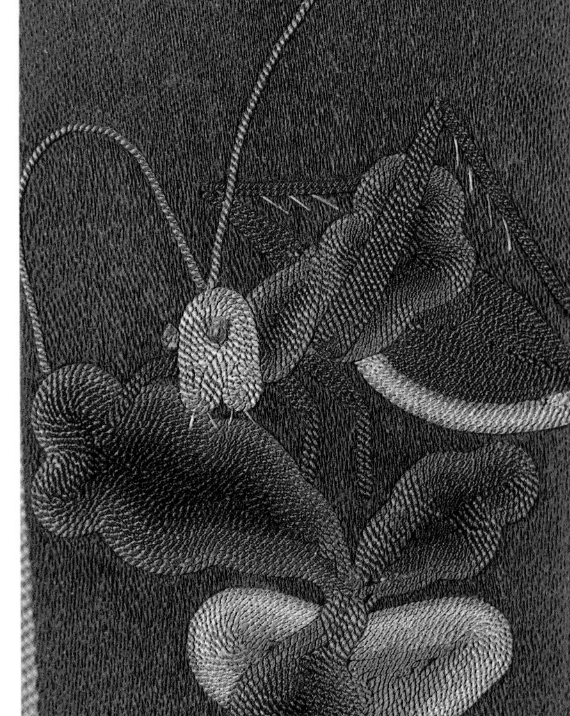

163

164

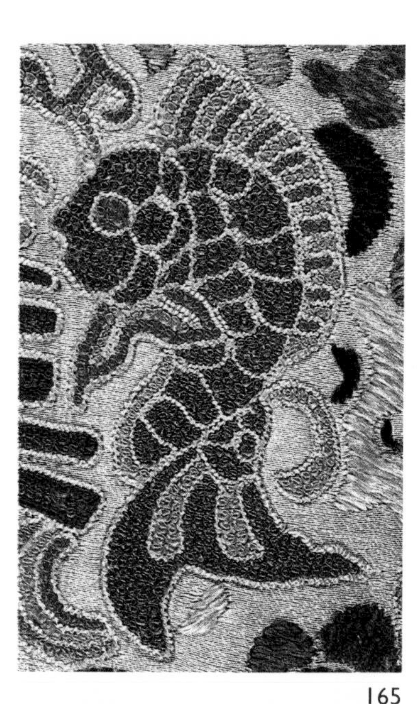

165

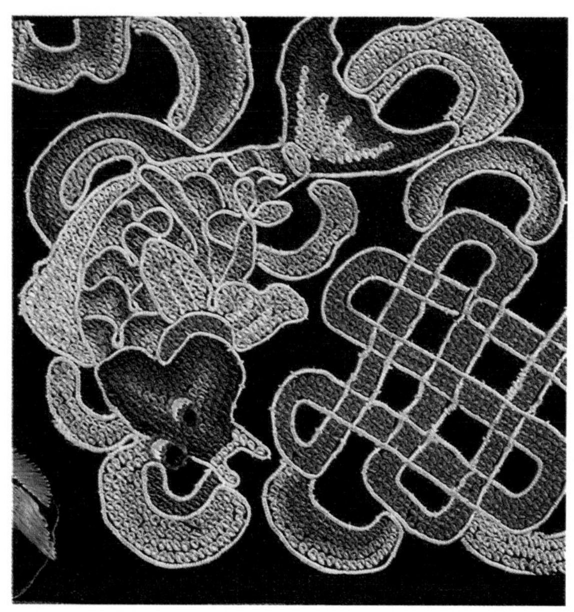

166

167

168

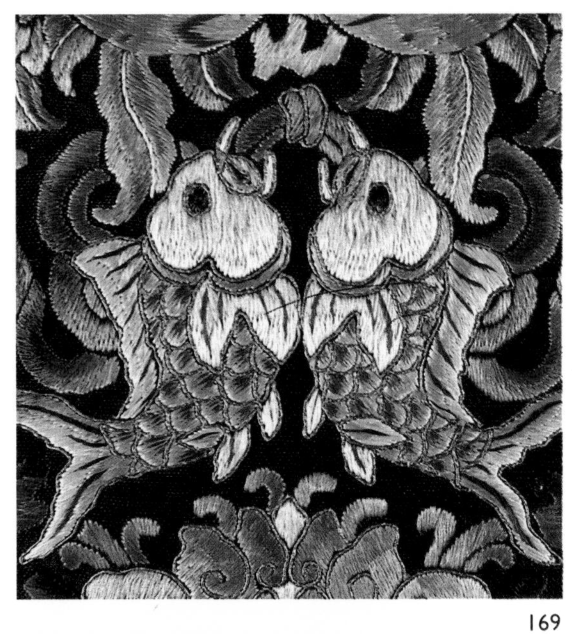

169

170

171

172

173

174

175

176

177

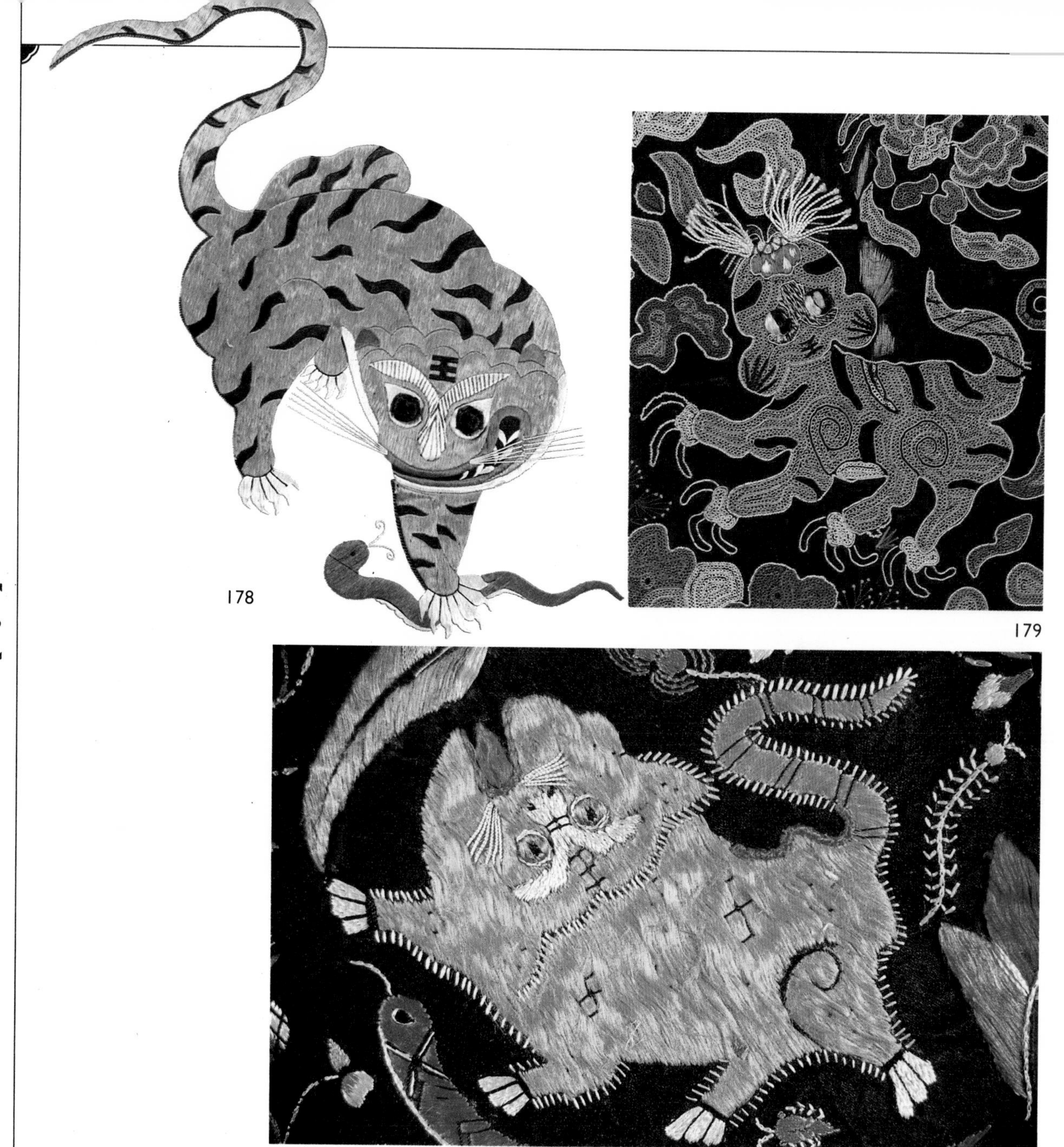

178

179

180

181

182

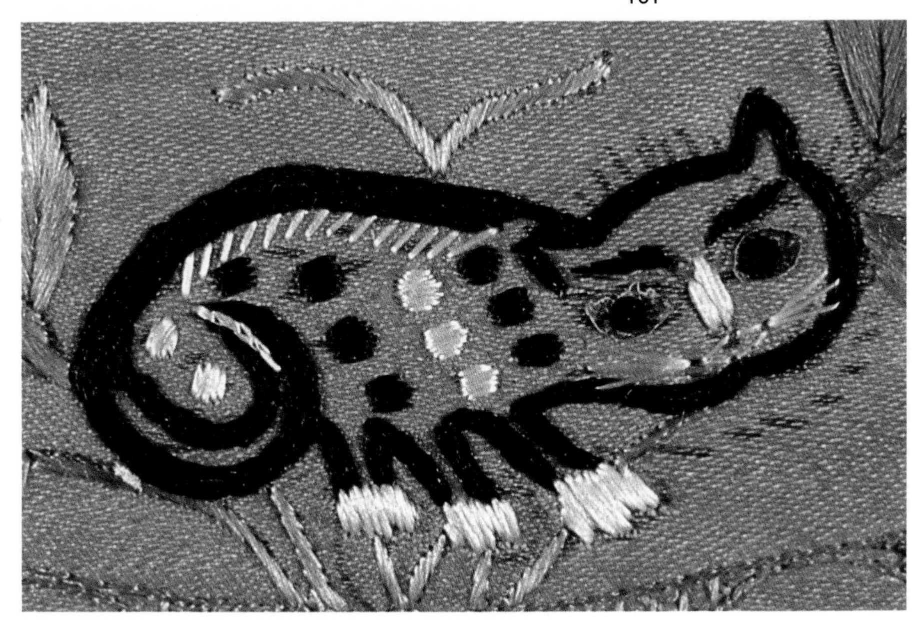

183

184

185

186

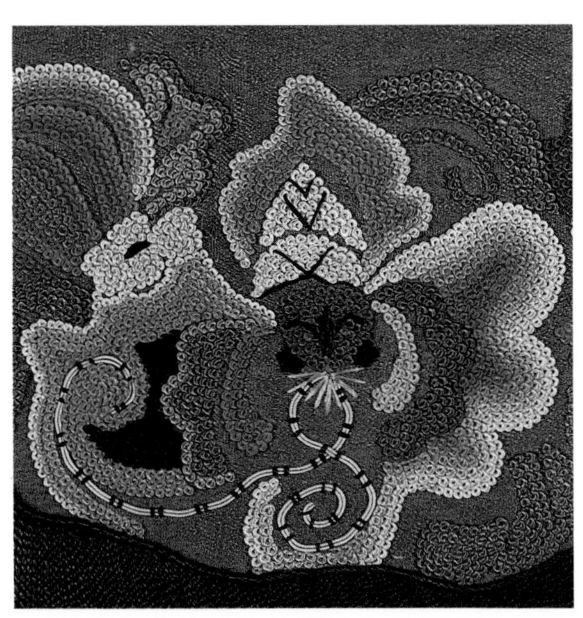

187

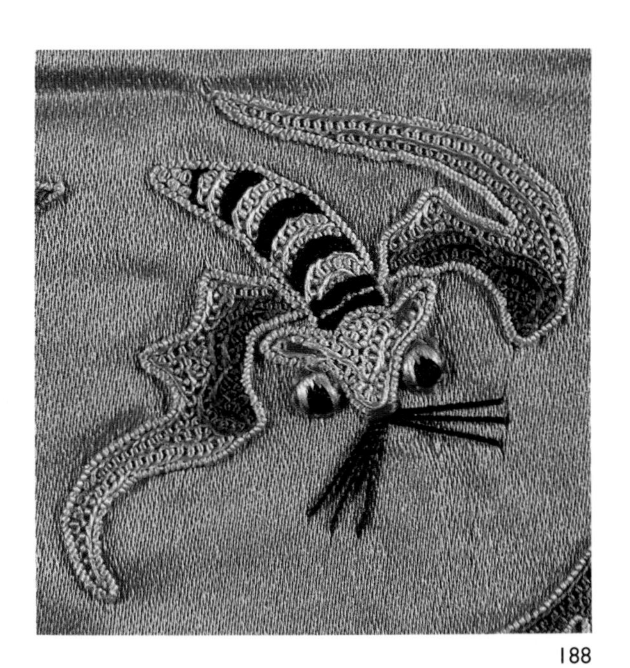

188

189

190

191

192

193

194

195

196

197

198

199

200

201

202

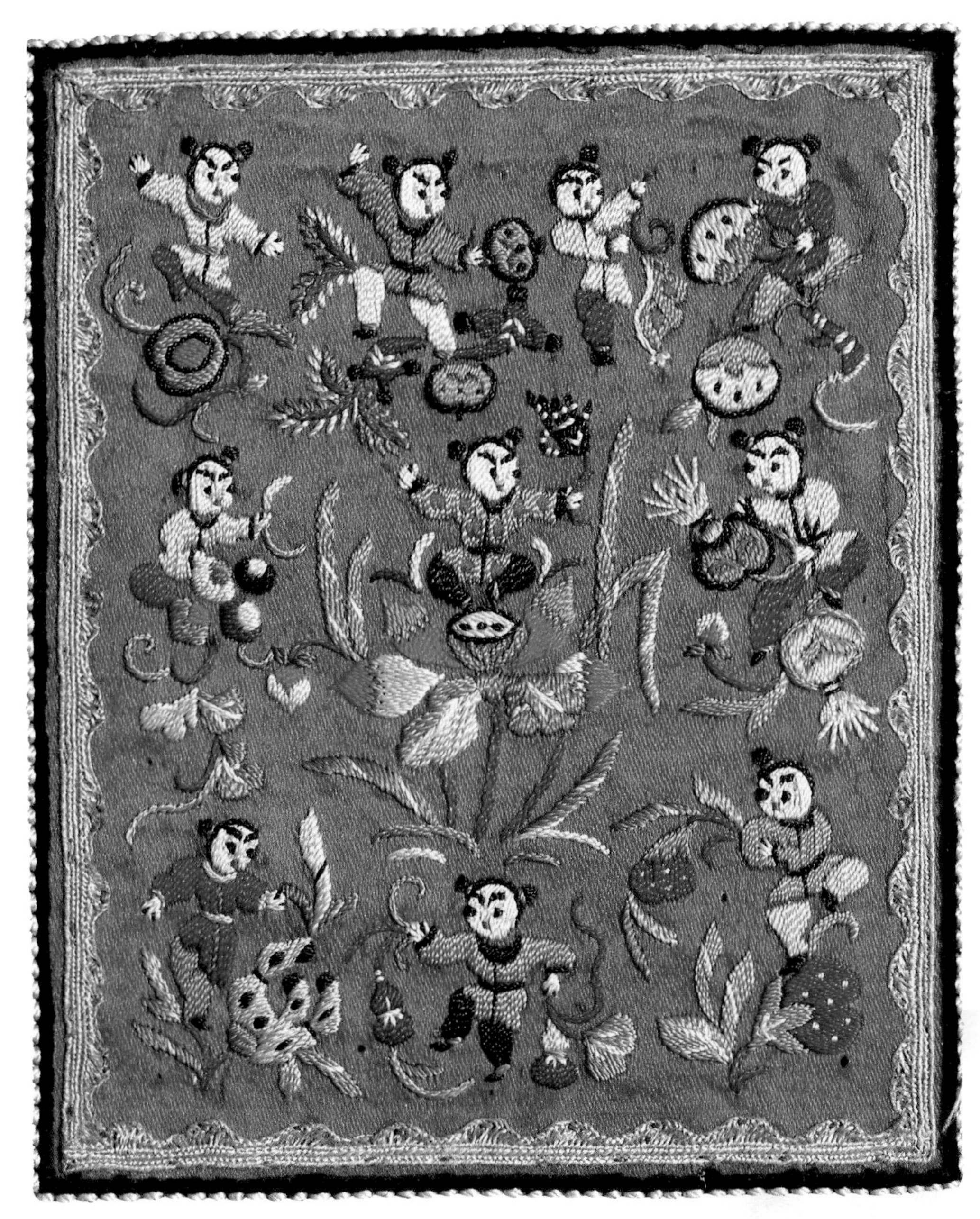

203

204

205

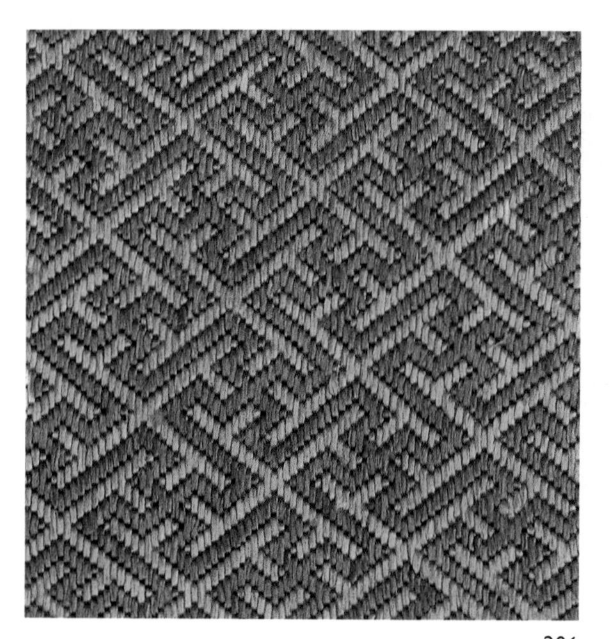

206

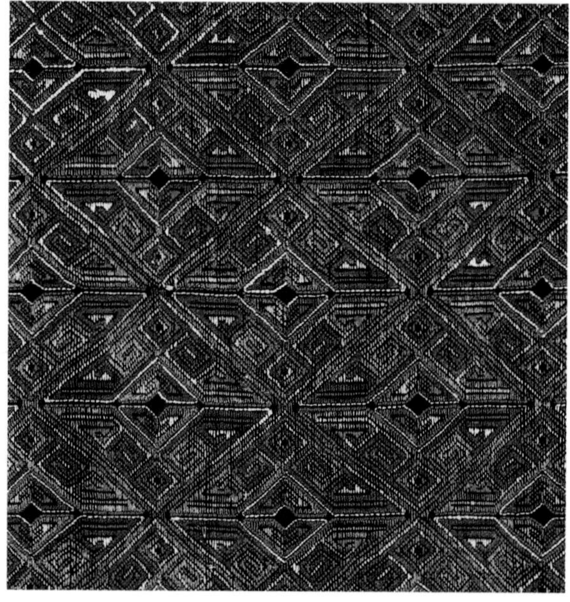

207

208

209

210

211

212

III. EMBROIDERY STITCHES

(A) The embroiderer's kit

1. Silk thread
2. Tailor's chalk line bag
3. Pin cushion
4. Embroidering frame
5. Cloth
6. Scissors
7. Unfinished embroidery work

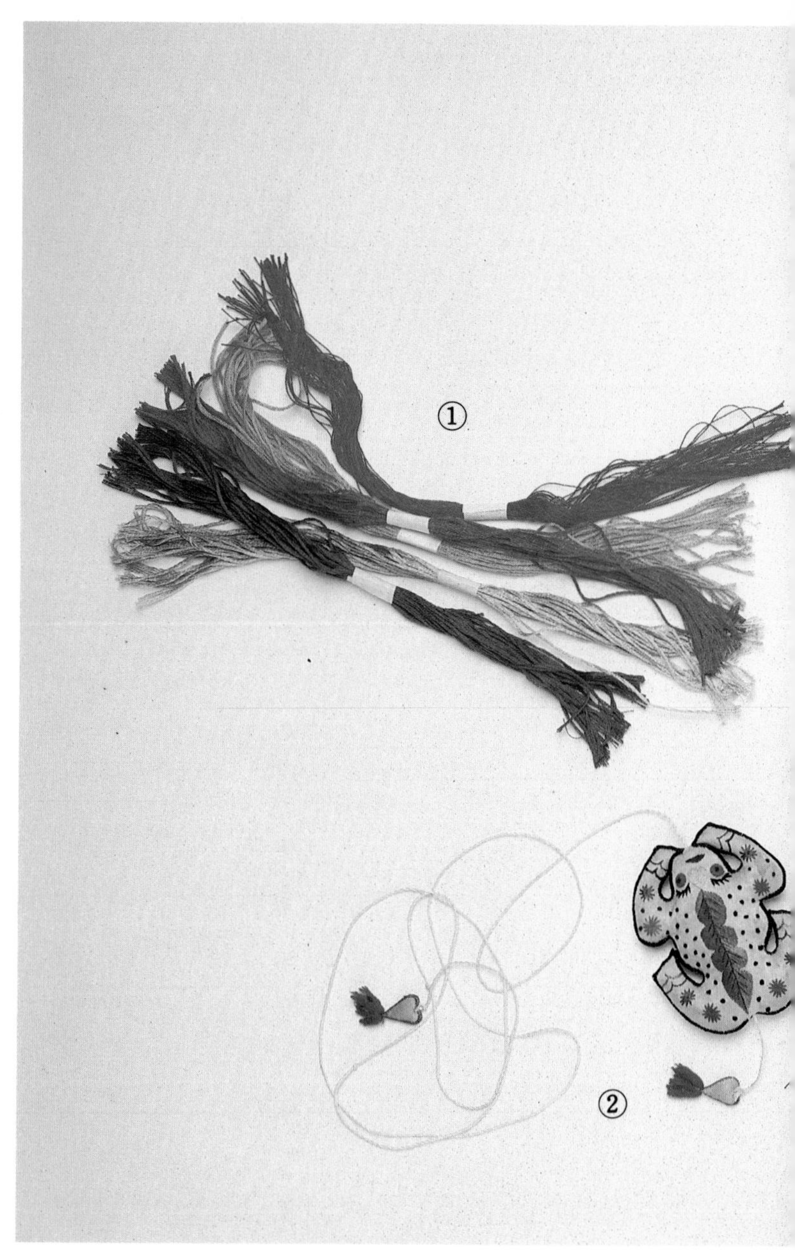

④
⑤
③
⑥
⑦

(B) The main stitches illustrated

Flat Stitchwork

The Satin Stitch (1), also known as Even Stitch or Beyond-the-edge Stitch, is a fundamental technique in embroidery in which the needle rises from one side of the design and falls on the other so that the space is filled in with neatly arranged stitches which do not overlap. It is often used to embroider tiny flowers or leaves. In embroidering larger patterns, the Satin Stitch is also used to form a ground layer before designs are wrought with other techniques, so that they look thick and attractive, and stitches that are too long can be firmly secured. Named by the different arrangements of threads, the varieties of the Satin Stitch include the Vertical Satin Stitch, the Horizontal Satin Stitch, the Slanting Satin Stitch and the Open Fishbone Stitch.

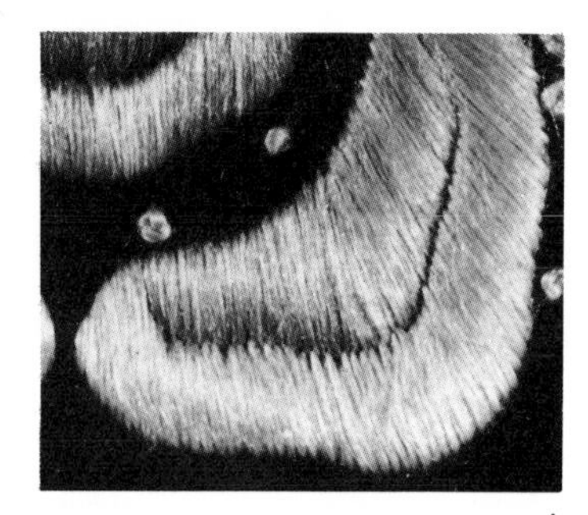

1

The Vertical Satin Stitch (2) runs vertically across the design.

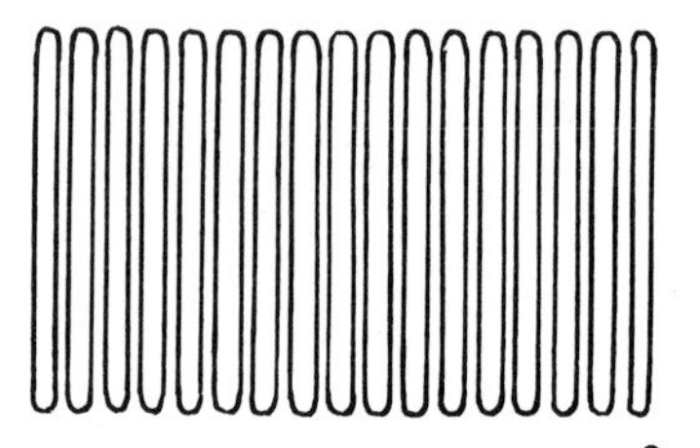

2

The Horizontal Satin Stitch (3) runs horizontally from one side of the design to the other.

3

The Slanting Satin Stitch (4) slants up or down from left to right, generally at an angle of 45 degrees.

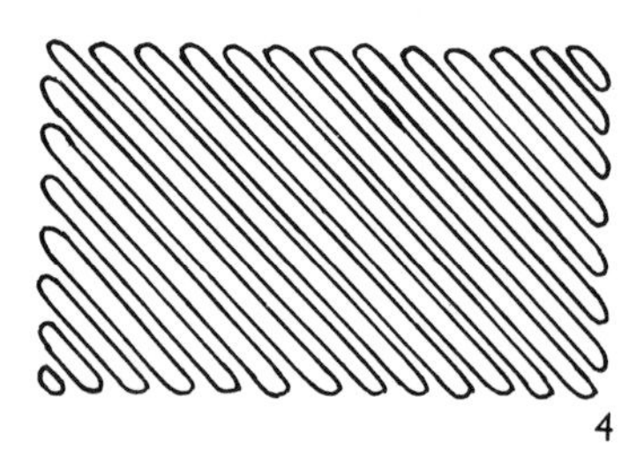

4

The Open Fishbone Stitch (5) goes from left to right, first slanting up and then down to form an inverted "V". It is often used to embroider branches and leaves of trees or the feathers of birds.

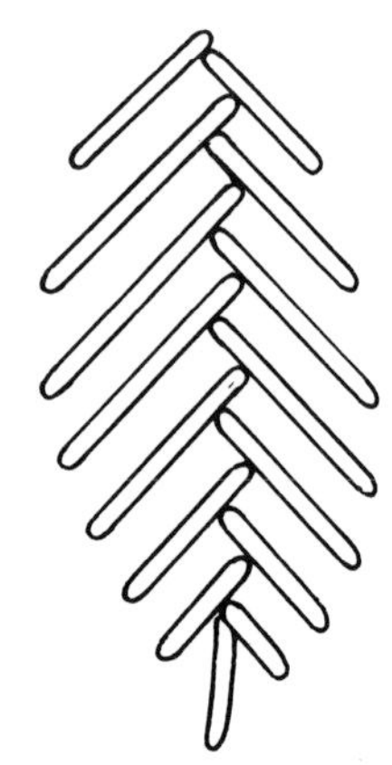

5

The Close-knit Stitch is a commonly used flat-stitching technique. The earliest embroideries exhibiting this skill were found in a Han tomb at Mawangdui, Changsha. It became very popular in the Song and Tang dynasties. The stitches can be flexibly arranged to facilitate colour-blending. The lines turn in a natural manner, suitable for harmonizing threads of different colours in *jiese* (joining one colour to another) and *xiangse* (adding a colour to another for matching or bringing the colour out). The Close-knit Stitch features in designs blazing with colours. It is mostly employed in pictures as well as in making reversible Suzhou embroideries. Varieties include the Single Close-knit Stitch, the Double Close-knit Stitch and the Multiple Close-knit Stitch.

The Single Close-knit Stitch (6) is also known as the Long-and-short Stitch. The Stitches are somewhat longer and the threads used are heavier. The method is generally used for embroidering flowers.

6

The Double Close-knit Stitch (7) is a method in which the stitches are even longer than those of the Single Close-knit Stitch so that they overlap each other. Layer after layer of stitches are tightly knitted together. The stitches are shorter where the line turns to facilitate colour-blending. The skill is suitable for embroidering forms of different objects.

The Multiple Close-knit Stitch is used

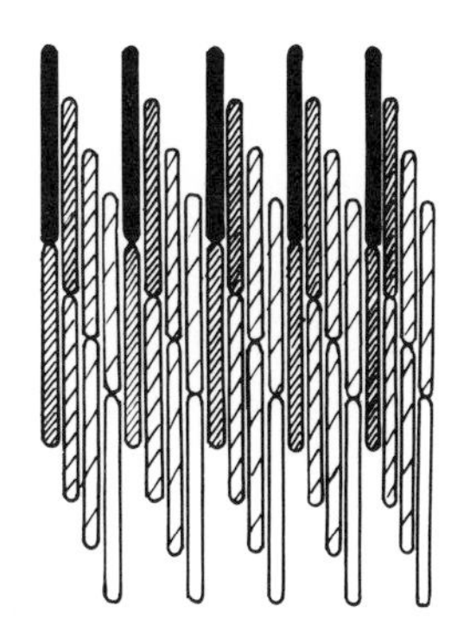

7

to embroider circular decorative designs and tiny round flowers. Stitches of equal lengths are arranged in such a manner that they appear to be radiating from a centre. The outermost layer of stitches should be executed first. Layer after layer of stitches are then added, with each layer getting progressively nearer the centre. The stitches of the innermost layer should focus on the centre of the circle.

With the **Layered Short-straight Stitch,** or *Qiang* Stitch, designs are formed by layers of closely joined short straight stitches. (In some places, "layer" is translated as *pi*, meaning "skin".) There are two ways of working. One can either begin with the outermost layer, working towards the centre (8) or vice versa. They are named the Inward Layered Short-straight Stitch and the Inverse Layered Short-straight Stitch respectively. With the inverse method, the border of each layer is clearly trimmed with a thread to make the layers even and tidy. The colours of the thread used should conform to the requirement of the designs, changing from darker colours to lighter ones to achieve the shading effect. Embroideries made using this technique are durable, as well as highly decorative. When designs intersect or overlap, the embroiderer usually leaves a narrow strip of unembroidered space inbetween called "voiding".

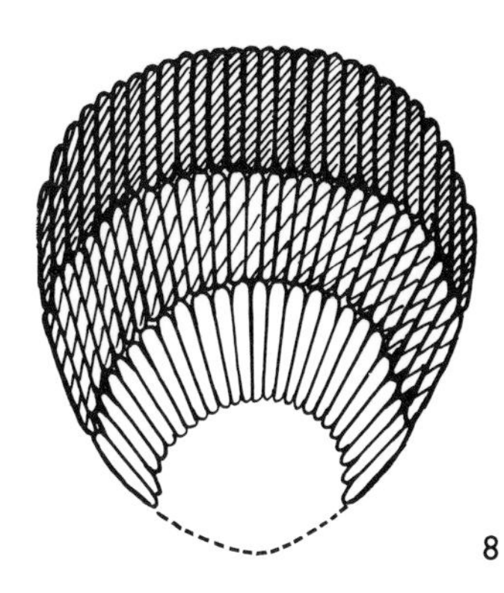

8

The Mixed Straight Stitch (9) or the *Chan* Stitch is capable of blending and harmonizing different colours to make the various tones shade into the same colour. The method is generally used to embroider flower petals and pistils. Long and short straight stitches are used alternately in the course of embroidering. They radiate from the centre, with the working stitches starting from the middle parting of the previous worked stitches and spreading out, so that there is no demarcation line between the layers. In the designs, the colours of threads used are optional, graduating either from a darker to a lighter tone or vice versa. This method can produce patterns which look

9

natural and realistic and is therefore often used for embroidering large flowers.

In **the Winding Stitch**, short slanting stitches pass through the cloth from the back, run across the area and return to the back of the work in a winding manner. Thus the designs have clear-cut edges, with stitches neatly and closely arranged. Both the surface and the back of the embroidered work look the same. Though this is a popular technique, it is not suitable for colour-blending. When embroidering, one only uses monochrome thread or thread that is capable of showing the graduated tones of a certain colour. The skill is therefore often used to delineate regular-shaped vigorous petals and leaves and vibrant lines like long chrysanthemum petals and the strokes of Chinese characters.

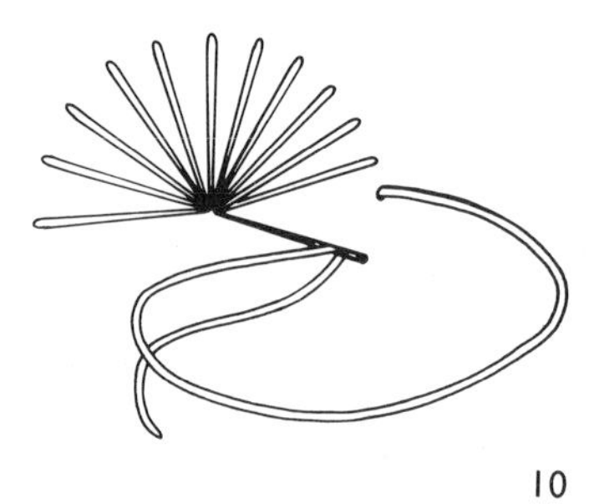

10

The Pine-needle Stitch (10) radiates like the ribs of a fan or the spokes of a wheel. All the stitches start from the circumference of a circle and end at the centre. In the north of China, it is popularly called *Basongmi* (forming the pine-needles) or *Bachegulu* (forming the wheel).

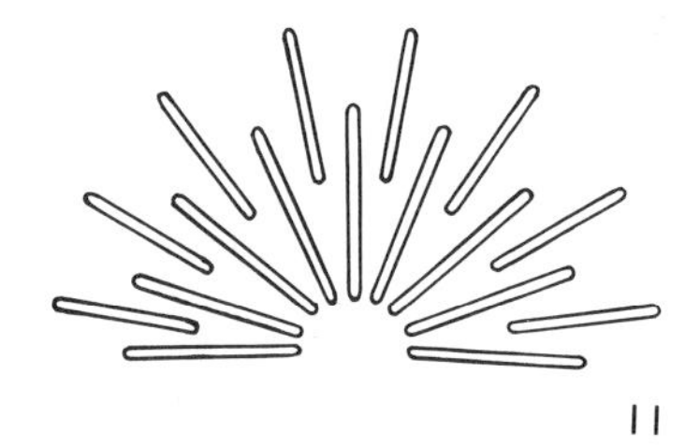

11

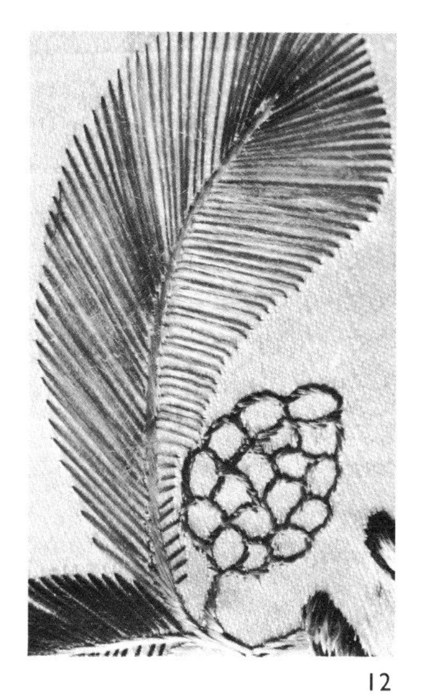

12

Scattering Stitches are either spread out as shown in (11), or appear like the vane of a feather with its hair slightly spreading out on the outer skirt but more concentrated on the rachis, as illustrated in (12). This technique is generally employed to embroider feathers or tree-leaves. In some places it is also called the "spreading-out stitch".

13

The Vortex-like Pattern Stitch (13) is called Shunxian (smoothly arranging the threads). The lines are arranged in a twisting round or radiating manner. Good effects can be achieved through the proper arrangement of the threads; the stitches can be either long or short, namely the "long extending stitches" and the "short extending stitches".

The Embroidering of Lines

The Stern Stitch (14) is used to describe tensile lines and appears like a twisted string when finished. It is also called the Rolling Stitch. The stitches twine round and press against each other, with each individual stitch working from a starting point of the previous stitch (its distance from the back of the preceding stitch should be 1/3 of its length); winding round and extending, the holes made by the needle are thus concealed. As the line formed is neither too heavy nor thin, it is often used to embroider tree branches, midribs of leaves, and edges of patterns or forceful lines.

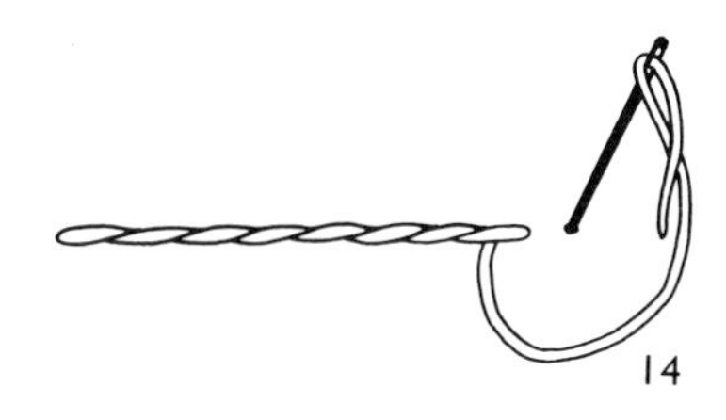

14

The Laced Back Stitch (15) is called the *Biao* (binding) Stitch. First embroider with Back Stitch, then lace with a different colour thread and draw it taut. It produces a similar effect to the Stern Stitch, but is more durable. In the northeast of China the technique is usually used to embroider pillow slips and door curtains. When two threads of contrasting colours are used, the resulting lines will even be more striking.

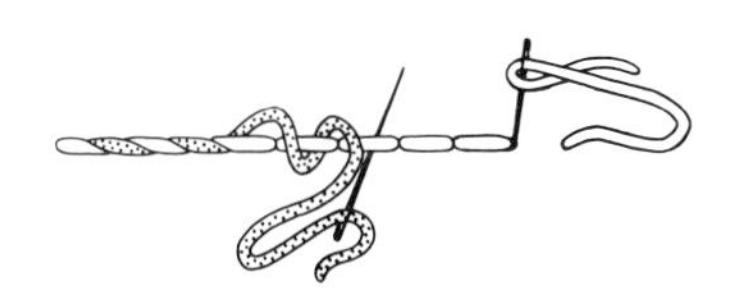

15

The Back Stitch (16) is also called the *Ji* Stitch. It is a commonly used method in which a backstitch meets the previous stitch at its starting point. Thus the line formed is as neat as if it had been drawn by a marker. The stitch type can be made very thin to describe the curved or long-and-fine lines used for fish fins, hair, landscapes and vines. It is also used for depicting transparent gauze or thin mist. Generally speaking, it is only used to supplement other methods owing to its apparent stitch holes.

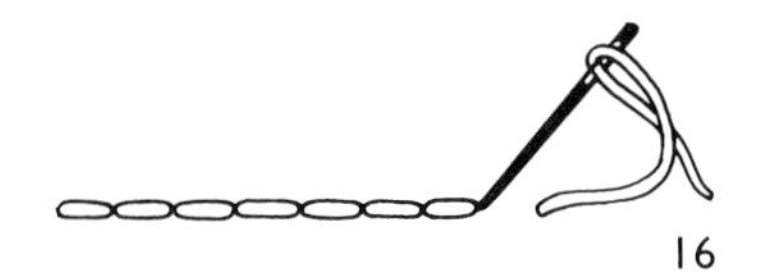

16

The Running Stitch (17) is called the *Gong* (pushing) Stitch. It is a fundamental skill in embroidery, used to fill in empty space. This technique is extremely simple. One needs only to push the needle through the cloth, and the stitches should be evenly spaced out at regular intervals.

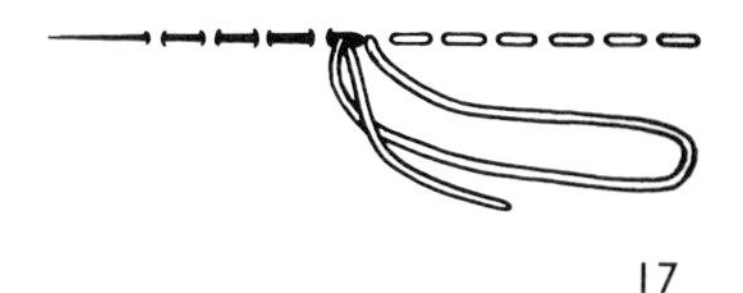

17

Couching

Couching (18, 19) involves the overlaying of a heavy single or double thread in a pattern and then fastening it down with fine stitches.

The thread used for fastening is thinner and its diverse colours help to vary the tone of the overall design. In order to distribute the colours evenly, the fastening stitches must be equally spaced and uniform in length.

The names of couching methods vary with the different threads being used. For instance, when gold or silver thread is used, it is called "couching of gold thread" or "couching of silver thread". When gold or silver thread (single or double thread) is used only to form the edge of a design, it is called *Quanjin* (circling with gold), which helps to trim the design to make it stand out and sometimes to harmonize with the adjacent contrasting colours. When a design is completely overlaid with gold thread, it is called *Panjin* (filling with gold).

When the colour of the thread used for fastening the gold or silver thread is varied, it will enable the metallic thread to reflect different colours and help to soften the harsh light emitted by the metal. Silk thread, thin thread, palm fibre (20) or horse-tail thread can also be used for couching.

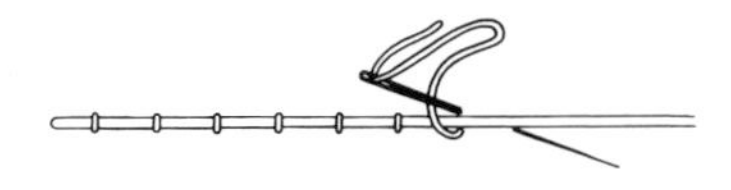

18

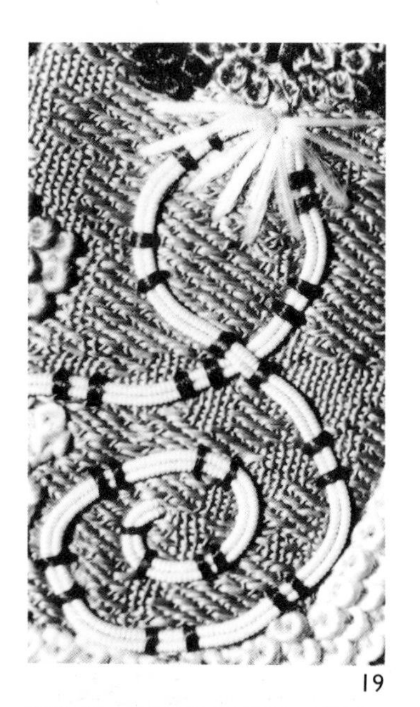
19

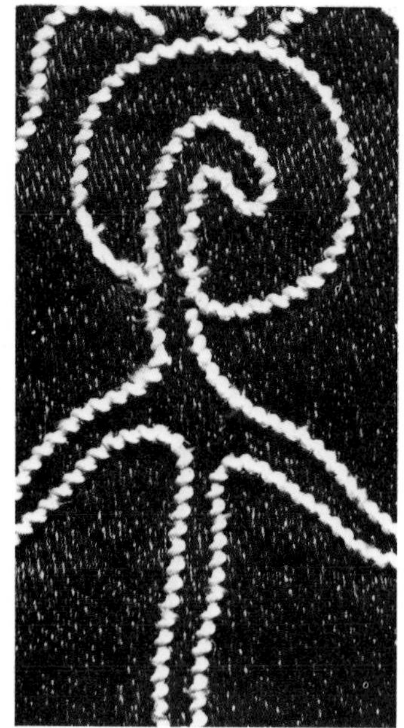
20

The Fastening Stitch (21, 22) is a method in which long Satin Stitches are fastened down with one or more straight or slanting short stitches. The purpose is to fix the long stitches as well as to enhance the artistic effect. It is a method extensively used.

21

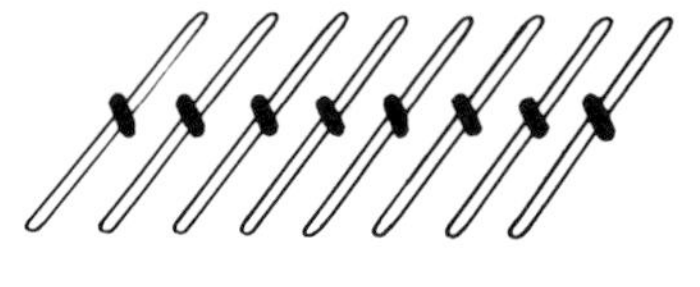
22

Pattern-shaping

The Fur-simulation Stitch is a technique widely used to embroider the fur of beasts or the feathers of birds. It can produce a striking decorative effect and is easy to work with. When embroidering, the ground is firstly covered with spreading stitches, and heavier threads should be used if the designs are in relief. After the groundwork is done, use thin threads to make hairlike short straight stitches mixed with various lengths to depict fur or feathers, embroidered by scattering stitches. The stitches can be either densely or thinly spread. There is no need to fill in the ground as long as they can resemble the quality of fur or feathers. The short stitches used help in fixing and holding down the long stitches in the groundwork.

Used to embroider eyebrows and eyelashes, the **Eyebrow and Eyelash Stitch** (23, 24) is called *Bayanjiemao* (making eyelashes). Since it is simple to work with, it is extensively used in folk embroidery.

23

24

The Binding Stitch is called the *Le* (curbing) Stitch. It is used to embroider the claw of a bird. First the groundwork is laid by means of Straight Satin Stitches. Then they are bound by horizontal stitches which form the shape of the bird's claw.

The Scale-carving Stitch is a method of depicting the scales of a fish and there are three ways: Scale-piling, Scale-laying and Scale-binding.

In **Scale-piling** (25), both long and short Close-knit Stitches are used. The scales thus formed are dark and dense inside with a lighter, thinner edge.

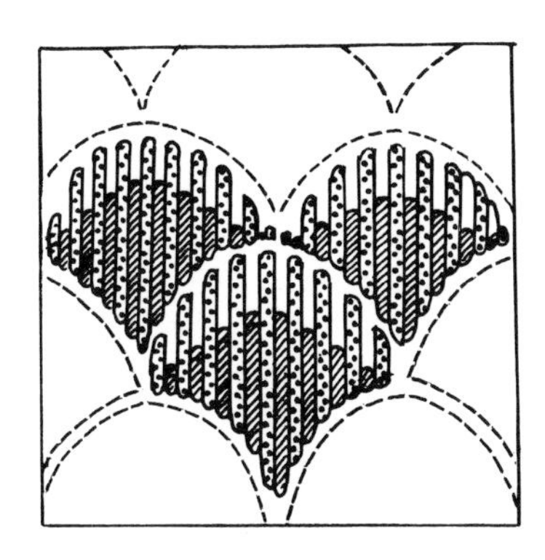

25

In the **Scale-laying** or *Qianglin* (scale-forming) Method (26), the scales are directly embroidered on the cloth in Layered Short-straight Stitches. No groundwork is needed, but one must leave "voiding" between the scales.

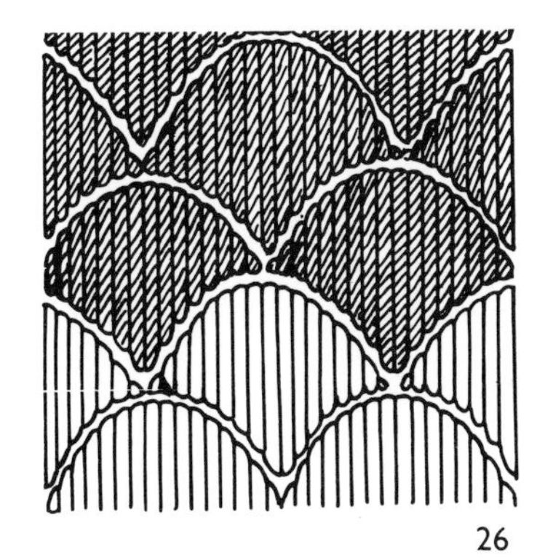

26

For the **Scale-binding** Method (27), first use straight stitches to form groundwork, which is then divided into scale-like sections by using Back Stitches.

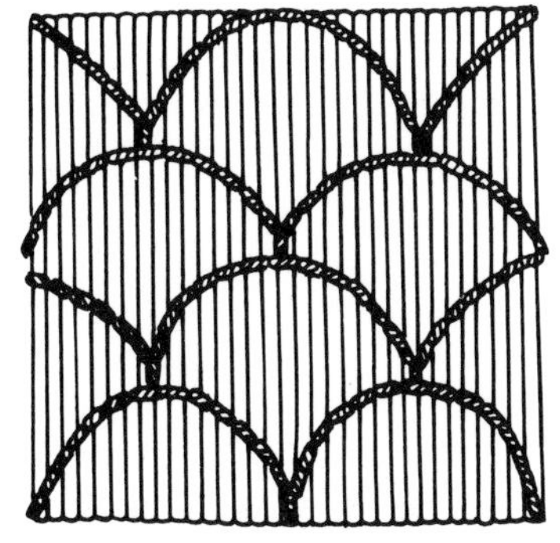

27

Darning Embroidery

Darning embroidery (28) resembles hand-weaving of weft-knit brocade. It is also called *Purong* (covering an area with stitches). To embroider, first lay warps of twisted yarn or silk floss on the ground material, then use split silk floss as wefts to form geometric designs extending symmetrically from the middle to both sides. Large flowers too can be embroidered in this way. Bright colours are generally used. When it comes to changing colour threads, the technique resembles that involved in the making of *Zhuanghua* (brocade with flower patterns).

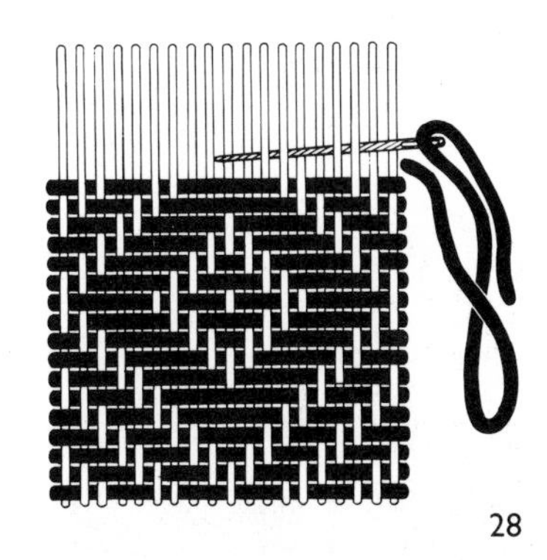

28

Lay-in Brocading or *Jiajin* (29, 30) is also called the *Puyu* (fish-spreading) Stitch. It features a ground fully covered with designs, mostly in geometric forms. Before embroidering, designs are drawn in the shape of squares, triangles or rhombuses and then embroidering is begun simultaneously from both sides with colour threads, which overlap and cross each other until the space is filled in.

29

30

Weave-in Embroidering

Gauze-embroidering (31, 32) is called *Nasha* or *Chuanhua* (weaving-in of patterns). Designs are made by passing colour threads through the meshes of a plain-coloured ground fabric, until it is entirely covered with designs. Sometimes the ground is only partially covered; this is known as *Chuosha* (jabbing the fabric). Some say these two methods are actually the same thing, called different names by northerners and the southerners. Gauze-embroidering first took shape in the Song dynasty. Some fine work was produced by this method in both Yuan and Ming days, and it became very popular under the reign of Jiaqing in the Qing dynasty.

To embroider, first draw designs on the back of the cloth. Next, stitch according to the designs already drawn so that patterns show on the right side. Split floss can be used for embroidering and the thickness of the threads should conform with the size of the meshes of the ground material. The skill is simple and easy. The thread can pass through the mesh in any manner (perpendicular, transverse or slanting). In order to achieve a pleasing decorative effect, the thread must not be drawn too tightly or too loosely, to avoid damaging the meshes or causing wrinkles on the surface.

31

32

The *Na* Stitch (sewing very close stitches) is done on a ground already covered with stitches. The designs, which consist of patches of colour, are made with double-thread and cover the whole ground. The embroideries achieved using this technique are very durable. They can be washed without causing the thread to break or fray. Pillow slips, curtains, table-cloths and door-curtains are usually embroidered by this method.

Pulling Embroidery

The Pulling Stitch (33, 34) is also known as the Silk-locking Stitch. When embroidering, two threads are used simultaneously. One thread is passed through the cloth from the back, the other thread is passed in the same manner at a point quite near the first stitch. The first thread is then wound round the second needle in a counter-clockwise direction to form a loop and then a backstitch is made by means of the second thread to fix the existing loop. After this, the second thread is once more passed through the cloth, and a loop made with the first thread winding in a counter-clockwise direction and the loop fastened with the second thread as before. This is repeated continuously until the desired effect is achieved. So the first thread only coils on the surface of the cloth to form patterns, and does not show on the back of the ground material. The second thread, usually of a thinner type, serves only to fasten the loops. Changing the thickness and the colours of the threads can produce pleasing visual effects.

Using this stitch can produce both durable and beautiful results. It is therefore widely employed in making folk embroideries for everyday use.

If these two threads crisscross right and left to form two strings of loops (35, 36) secured on the ground material, the result is a **Double Pulling Stitch.**

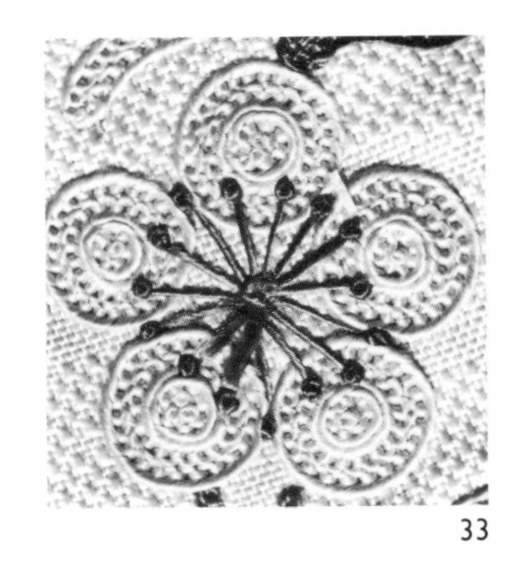

33

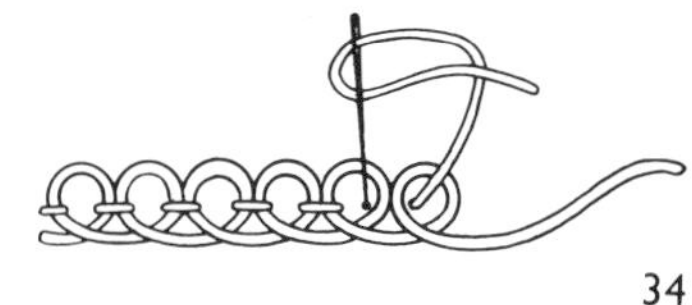

34

35

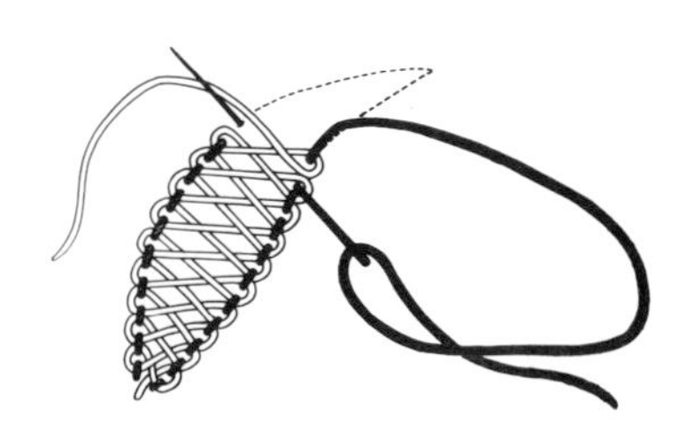

36

The Coiling Stitch (37, 38) is another form of Pulling Embroidery, also made with two threads. One thread coils to form designs fastened by the other by means of a back-stitch. Thick double-thread is used for coiling, while thinner thread is used to fix the patterns in position. The embroidery is done with the help of a very thick thread or a tiny round stick that serves as a knitting-needle to form loops. After being detached from the thick thread or the stick, the loops are fastened and coiled into designs. The thread can be changed at will to give the desired effect. The technique, being time-consuming, is seldom used, but it has a very strong decorative effect not to be matched by other skills when used to embroider flowers in relief.

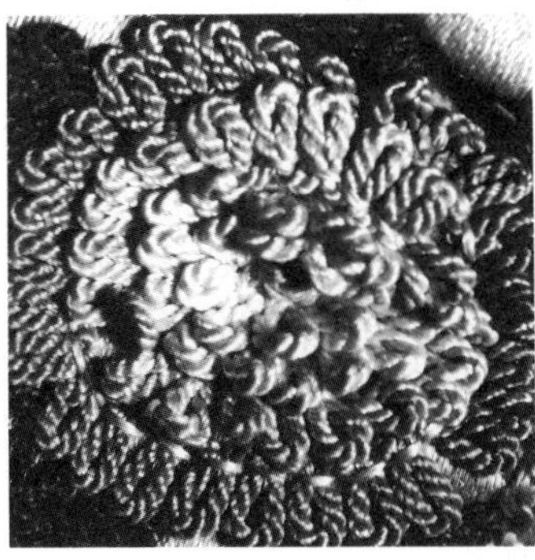

37

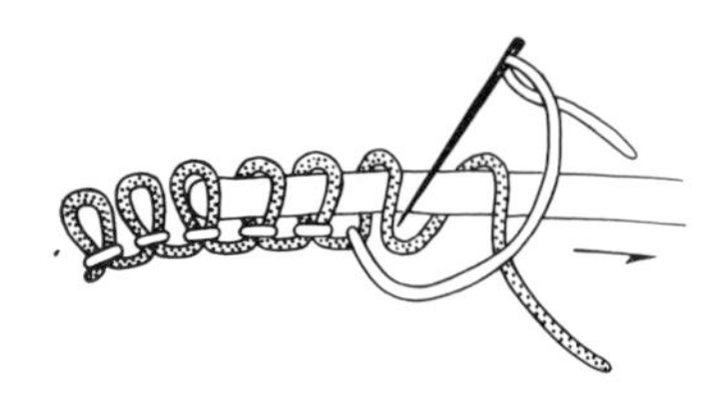

38

Chain Embroidery

The Chain Stitch (39) is also called the Linking Stitch or *Suohua* (locking of patterns). It is formed by rings of silk linked together in chains. The technique is simple and it is one of the oldest methods in Chinese embroidery. The earliest specimen found dates back to the Western Zhou dynasty. Later specimens discovered in a Western Han tomb at Dabaotai, Beijing, also clearly show chain stitches (40).

Because of its porous and consequently matt surface, the embroidery has a calm and dignified appearance which adds to the beauty of the picture as a whole. If Satin stitch-work made with split floss can be compared with Flashing Satin, then it will not be far wrong for us to liken embroideries done in Chain Stitch to Silk Gauze.

Though colours contrast more sharply in chain stitchwork than in satin stitchwork, after being blended they are never unpleasant to the eye. Patterns formed by this method are highly decorative, with resilient lines and clear-cut edges in relief. The embroidery is durable and washes well.

From this basic skill, there have evolved a number of variations:

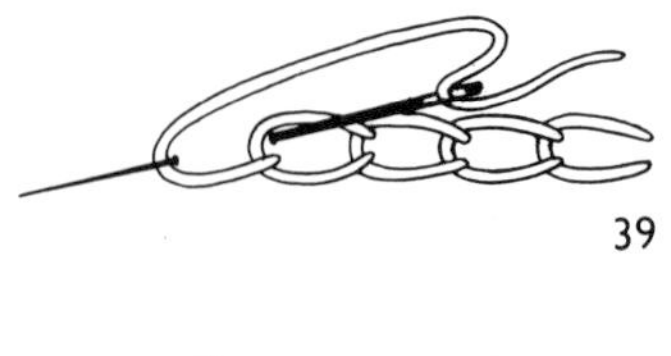

39

40

The Close-ring Chain Stitch (41) is a method in which the needle rises from and falls into the same needle-hole in the cloth to form chains of rings.

41

The Open-ring Chain Stitch (42) forms chains of rings with larger ring holes.

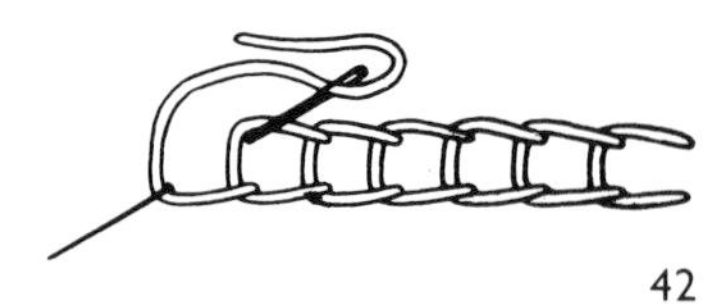

42

The Double-ring Chain Stitch (43) is a method whereby a chain with strongly locked edges is formed, in which two rings are fastened close together.

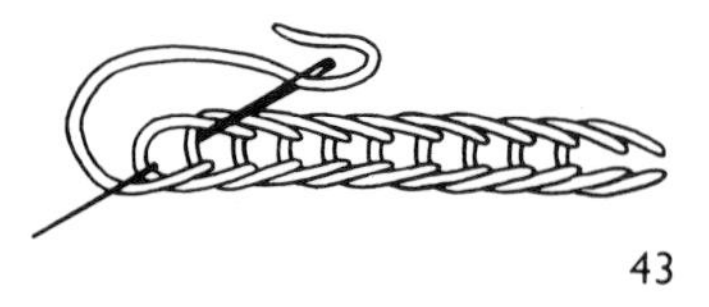

43

When rings are made separately instead of being linked together, they are called **the Daisy Stitch, the Detached Chain Stitch** or **the Single-ring Stitch** (44, 45). When these take the form of a curve crossing itself, they are called **Loop Stitches** (46).

44

45

46

The **Fly Stitch** or **the Half-ring Stitch** (47) and **the Feather Stitch** (48, 49) are variations of the Chain Stitch. They are made like the Chain Stitch, but their two ends are far apart. They can be made separately or joined together to form designs, which can be used for edging.

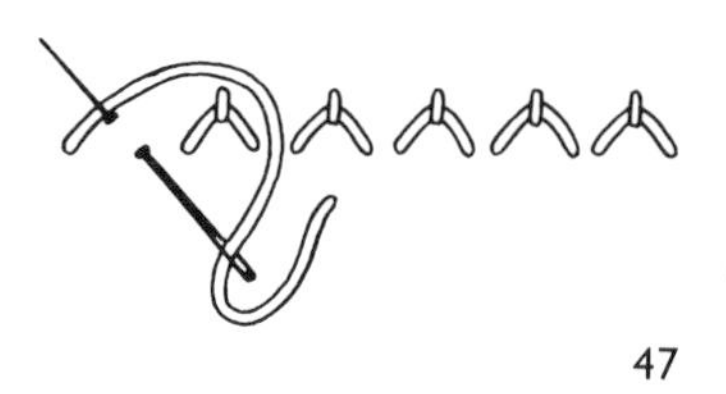

47

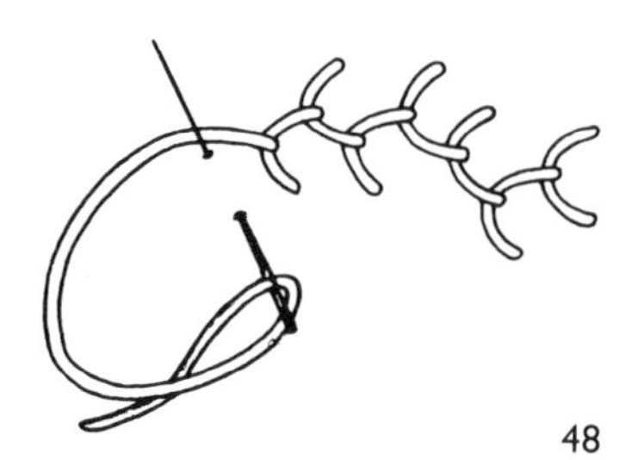

48

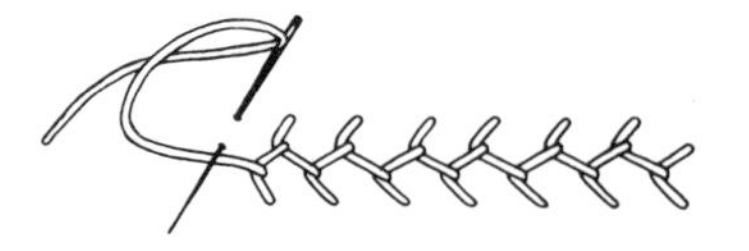

49

The Braid Stitch (50), otherwise known as Strands of Braids, is a kind of Chain Stitch. In this method the needle passes through the thread itself to form the first ring, instead of passing through the ring as in the Double-ring Chain Stitch, and connects the first ring with the second. This goes on until the rings are securely locked together like hair braids. The chain of stitches is usually made with heavy threads and used for edging. In this case, it is sometimes reinforced by another chain. When edging a long border, the embroiderer usually changes the colour of the thread section by section in accordance with the design. Symmetrical designs usually have edges on both sides. This is a method widely used among the Miao people in Guizhou.

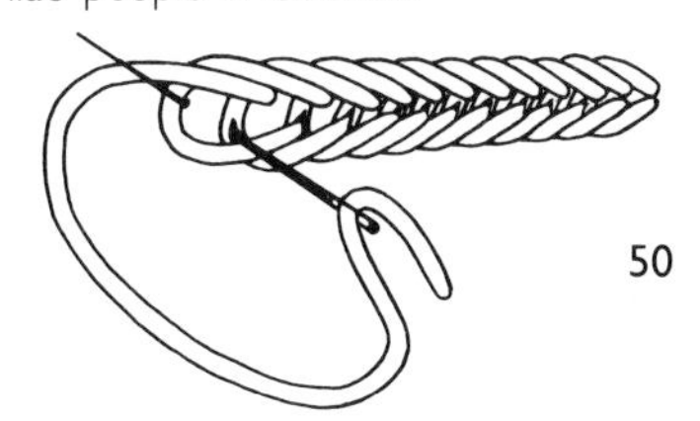

50

The Blanket Stitch (51) is also called the Edge-sealing Stitch or Button-locking. It is known as *Wenming* (elegant) Edge in Chinese. It is often used to embroider button-holes and edges of clothes, for making designs of small or medium size. It is also used in the *Baohua* (adding cutout patterns on the ground material and covering these with stitches) and carving methods. When the technique is used to fix a gold thread, it is called *Suojin* or the "locking of gold".

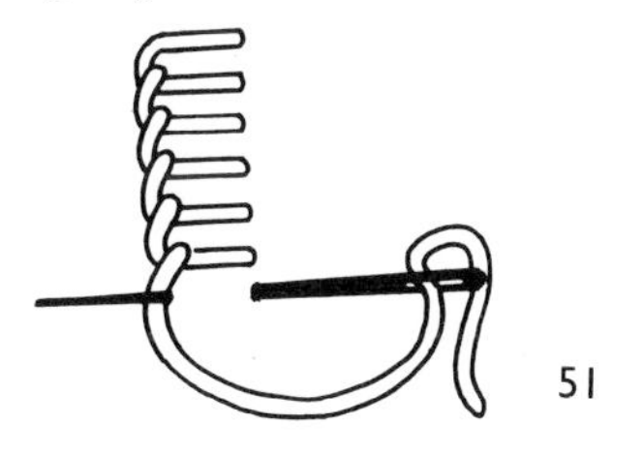

51

The Consecutive Stitch (52) is also called the Split Stitch. A backstitch passes through the end of the thread of the previous stitch and splits it in two. The effect achieved resembles that of the Chain Stitch, but the line is not formed by rings. This is in fact a simplified Chain Stitch (so it is popularly called the Fake Stitch). It can be used on its own; but in ancient times, it was often used together with the Chain Stitch to embroider thin lines.

52

Knotting

The Knot Stitch (53, 54, 55, 56) is also known as Ring Embroidering. It is a useful and simple method that forms designs in relief which have a shiny effect; the name was given because these designs are made of tiny knots on the ground material. The knots can be made in different ways. They can be big or small, and they can be very useful for forming patterns. The method is one of the oldest stitching skills and is extremely important in embroidery. Early relics done in this stitch were found in an Eastern Han tomb unearthed at Nuoyinwula, Mongolia. Even earlier specimens were the decorative knots on a pair of silk shoes discovered in a tomb of the Warring States Period in Linzi, Shandong Province. The skill is generally is used to embroider the pistils of flowers. It can also be used for animals, figures, and other designs; and it is particularly useful for objects which wear out easily, such as small bags, *Dalian* (bags sewn up at both ends with an opening in the middle), seat cushions and children's shoes. More than twenty varieties of stitch of this form can be found.

Four different kinds of Knot Stitches (56).

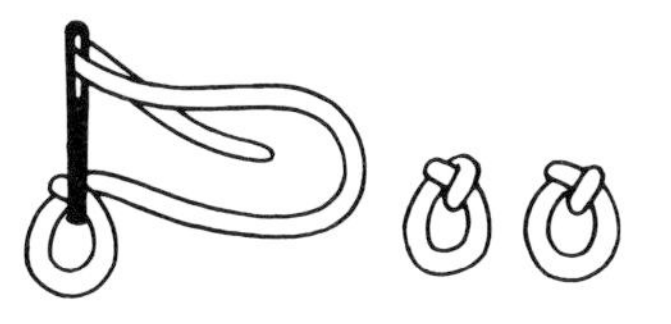

53

54

55

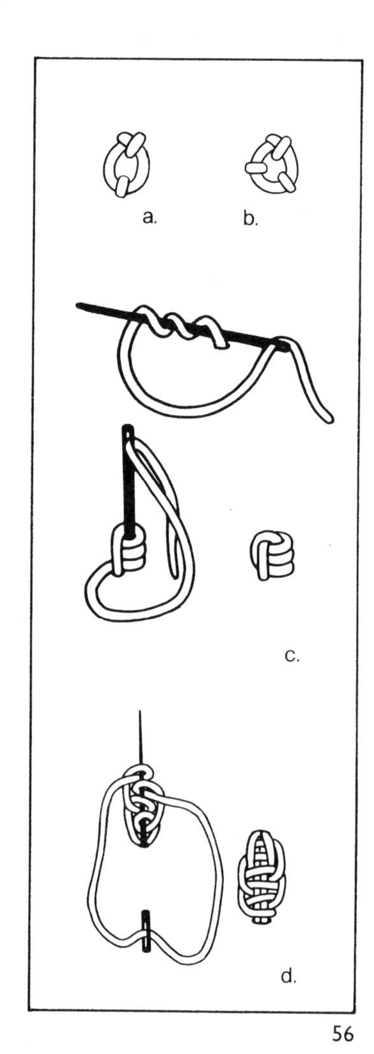

56

Netting

The Net Stitch (57, 58, 59, 60, 61, 62) (*see also* Plates No. 35, 42, 43) is also called *Huazhenxiu* or *Wenzhenxiu* (both meaning pattern embroidery). Among the Miao People, it is known as *Banhua* (pulling designs). Gauze with regular meshes may be used as the ground material, on which designs are embroidered by passing thread through the meshes. When tightly woven material is used, one can sew on threads to form straight lines, slanting lines, or checks, and then make further designs on top of them. When different designs are formed using the Net Stitch or when the designs are formed by the combined use of this stitch and other techniques, the net stitching parts should be surrounded by a border of Rolling Stitches or by Couching of gold or silver threads. As stated above, Net Stitching can be employed on its own or in conjunction with other methods to make beautiful patterns.

Designs worked on a material with meshes often give the effect of a hollowed-out carving. But when they are made on a closely woven fabric, they will appear as if covered with an extremely thin patterned curtain. The products are in great demand.

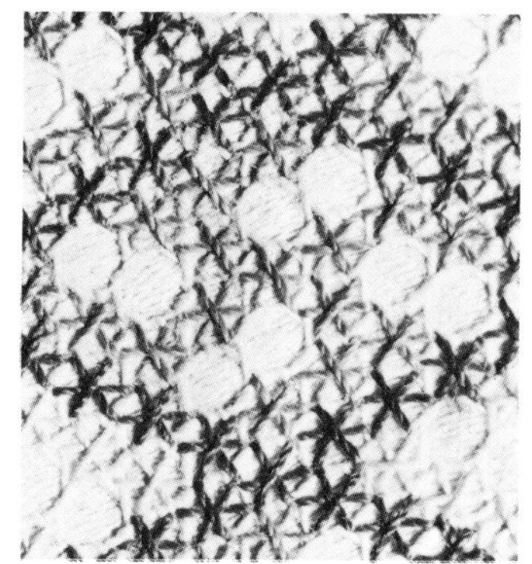

57

Net Stitching: Example 1 (See also Plate No.35)

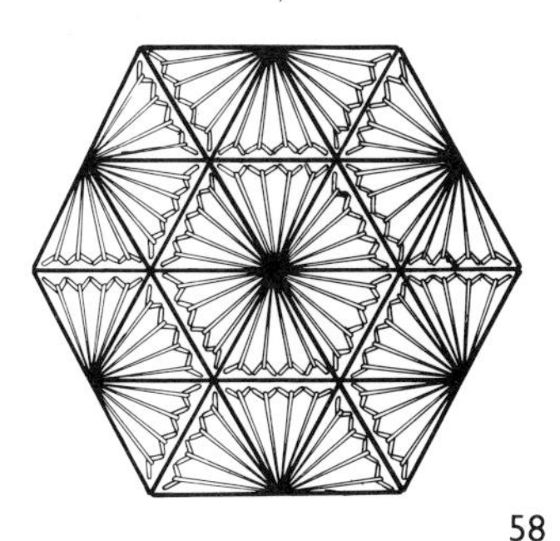

58

Net Stitching: Example 2 (See also Plate No.35)

59

Net Stitching: Example 3 (See also Plate No.35)

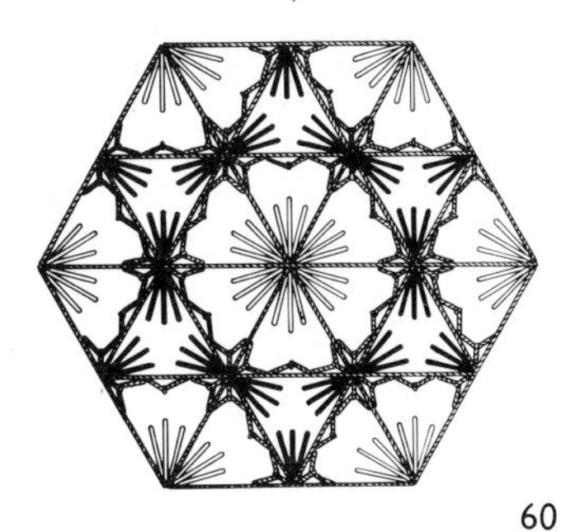

60

Net Stitching: Example 4 (See also Plate No.42)

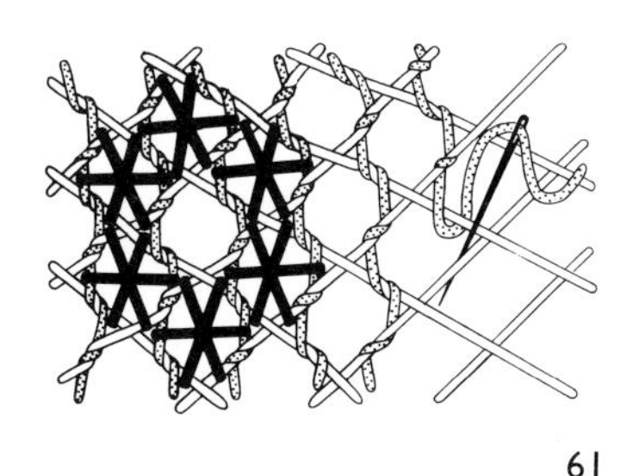

61

Net Stitching: Example 5 (See also Plate No.43)

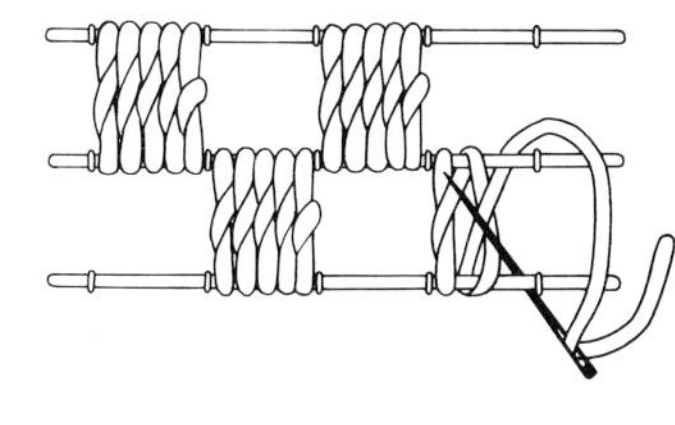

62

Cross Stitching

The Cross Stitch (63, 64, 65) is called *Tiaohua* (picking patterns) or *Tiaoluo* (stitching in gauze). It is an ancient technique which features designs formed by crosses. The number of crosses to be embroidered on the material is determined by its size. The crosses should be of the same size, neatly arranged and evenly spaced. Great care should be taken when passing the thread: if too much force is used, it will cause wrinkles on the surface of the ground material, but if the force applied is too small, the design will get out of shape and become furred. This will affect the appearance and durability of the embroidery. The Open Fishbone Stitch is also used on occasions, instead of the Cross Stitch, however it is not so popular owing to its rigidity.

Both monochrome and polychrome threads are used, but the monochrome type is more popular. The stitch is very widely used by the minority peoples in China. Aprons, pillow slips, and handkerchiefs used by peasant women are usually embroidered in this way. Embroidery of this kind is durable, highly decorative and easy to make.

63

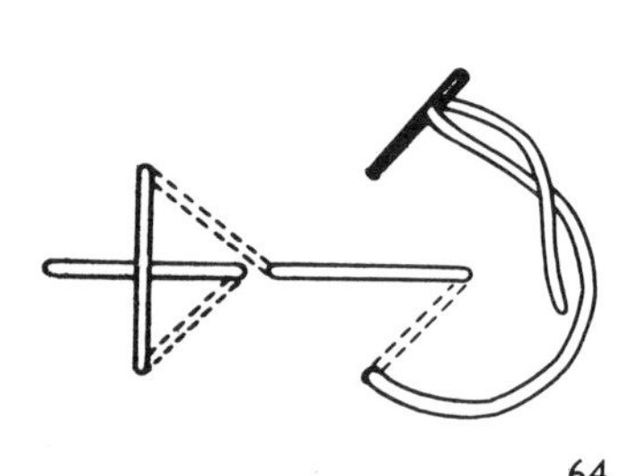

64

65

Edging

The method of **edging** can greatly improve the quality of an embroidery. Edges not only heighten the decorative effect of the designs but also make the embroidered work more durable, so they are therefore very important.

The edging skills used in folk embroidery are of all kinds (66, 67, 68, 69, 70, 71). The most popular ones are "hound's-tooth", "Cucumber trellises", "lotus leaves" and so on. There are also a lot of other more complicated methods.

Edging techniques:

Example 1 front, back (66)

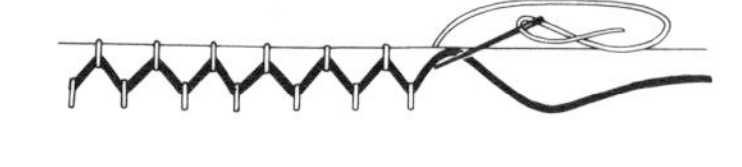

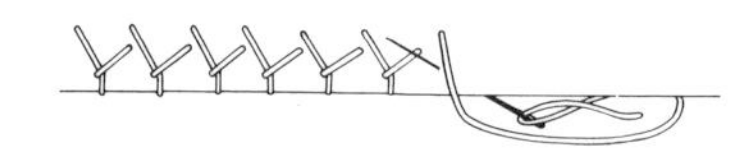

66

Example 2 lattice pattern (67)

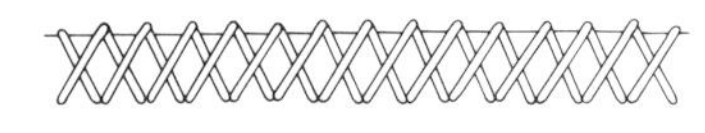

67

Example 3 hound's-tooth pattern (68)

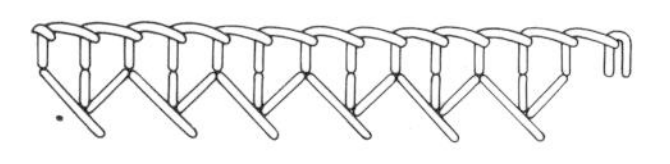

68

Example 4 Chevron Stitch (69)

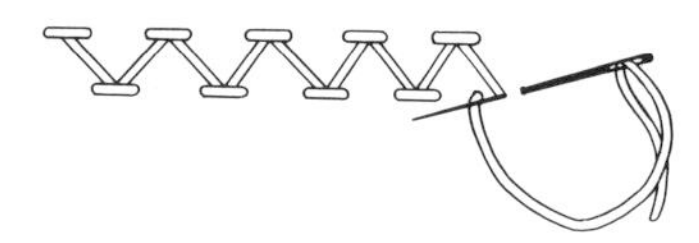

69

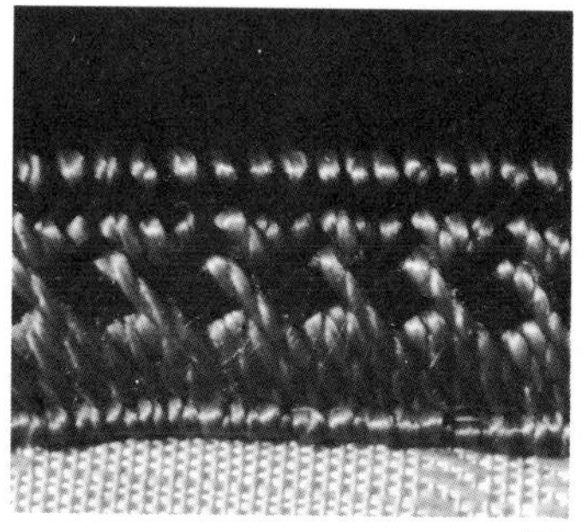

70

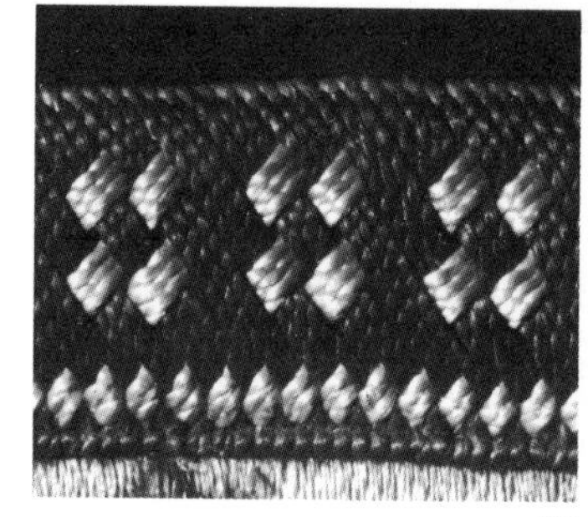

71

Other Skills

Appliqué is known as *Buhua* (patch pattern) or *Tieling* (adding damask silk); in other words, the addition of cutout designs made of exotic material onto the ground material. When cutout shapes serving as pads are laid under embroidery designs, the method is called *Baohua*. Before embroidering, patterns made of cotton or silk should be cut out and patched on the ground material by Edge-sealing Stitches or other straight stitches along their edges. The method, though very simple, can produce very attractive effects and is therefore widely used either on its own or in conjunction with other methods.

The Piling Method (72) is also called High-rising Embroidery or Padding. It is a method by which a part of the design is raised higher than the rest. This can be done by adding layers of heavy threads, cotton, or a pad of paper fastened with Long and Short Stitches. The raised part will then be covered with a layer of stitches to produce very realistic designs in relief.

72

The Carving Method (73, 74) is called *Diaoxiu*. Long stitches are firstly sewn around the edges of the design with a heavy thread. Next the heavy thread is covered up with Edge-sealing or Winding Stitches. In this way, the designs will be raised above the ground material. The parts to be hollowed are then cut out with a small pair of scissors. To add to the complexity of the design, one can put a piece of thin gauze over the hollow places or add designs in those areas by means of net stitching. This method can be used in different ways. The products are of two kinds: complete carving (with the entire design hollowed out) and partial carving (with the design partially hollowed out). Illustrations No.73 and 74 show a spectacle case. It is a complete carving, first embroidered with Knot Stitches and Couching of palm fibres and then the unwanted parts cut out according to the design of the pattern. Products usually look more beautiful, subtle and elegant when the colour of thread is the same as that of the ground material.

73

74

The Random Stitch is done with straight stitches, irregularly arranged to depict part of a design. It might have been invented to imitate the shaded parts in *literati* paintings. It is exemplified by the trees in a Song embroidered painting entitled *Riding a Crane over a Beautiful Terrace*, now preserved by the Museum of Liaoning Province.

Double-face Embroidery is also known as Two-face Embroidery. This is usually done with Close-knit Stitches. The places where the threads passed in and out of the ground material should be well concealed so that the same visual effect can be achieved on both sides. The embroideries done by the Miao people in Guizhou and Sichuan Provinces also show the same regular geometric patterns on both sides of the cloth. They call the method *Limianhua* (inside-pattern making) or *Xianhua* (small-pattern making). They use monochrome single threads as weft or warp to form elegant designs.

Shadow Embroidering is also called *Tuodixiu* (groundless embroidery). This is done on a piece of thin, transparent material. Stitches should be made on the back of the ground material with chosen patterns so that the embroidered design will show on the right side. This kind of embroidery is unique in terms of its artistic charm.

Ground-borrowing Embroidery is also known as *Jiedixiu*. The name itself means "supplementing the effect of the design by ground colour". In the course of embroidering, blanks are purposely left on the ground material so that they become part of the design.

Colour-borrowing Embroidery is also called *Jiesexiu* or "half-embroidery-half-painting", because parts of the design are painted with brushes. This method saves time and labour. Sometimes one only embroiders the major designs, leaving the rest to the painter. Sometimes only the outline of a pattern is embroidered. Sometimes colours are added to achieve the right tone for the picture. Many different methods are involved.

In **Gold-shadowing Embroidery,** or *Yinjin*, stitches are made on a design already covered with gold foil so that golden light will glisten forth between them to create an opulent look. This is a method widely used in Guangdong embroidery.

In **Core-wrapping Embroidery,** the *Baogeng* method (75) is combined with the Button-hole Stitch (76) or the Eyelet Holes (77), depending on the design chosen. Running stitches should be made on the ground material with very thick core thread. Cores made of other materials can also be used. Silk threads are wound or wrapped around the core by means of Edge-sealing Stitches. The embroidered lines then rise in relief. Care should be taken not to draw the thread too tight or too loose. It will become a carved embroidery when the design is "hollowed".

Fastening a heavy core line (75).

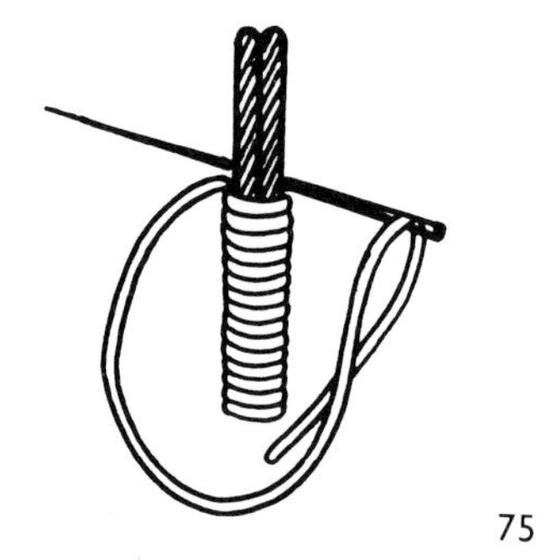

75

Wrapping the core line with stitches (76).

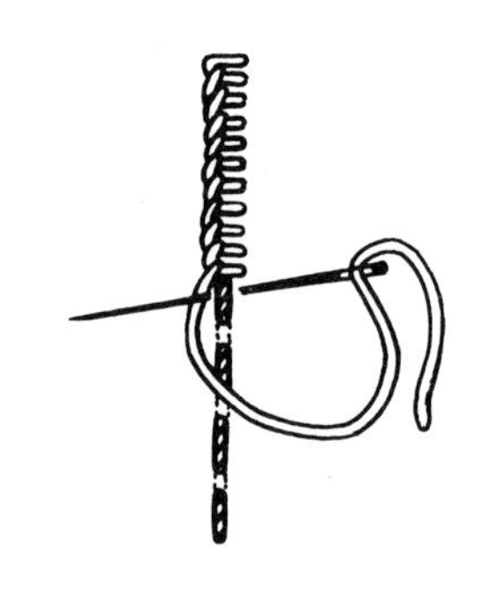

76

Wrapping the core line with stitches (77).

77

Woollen yarn can be used in embroidering instead of silk floss. Coarse linen is normally used for the ground. The designs are made by the Gauze-embroidering method, passing the yarn through the meshes of the ground material. Embroideries thus made are durable, and a great favourite in general.

For **Wool-cutting Embroidery,** or *Jianrongxiu*, a special needle (a large syringe needle can be adapted to this purpose) is used. The needle and yarn pass through the ground material from the back and make Close-knit Stitches along the edge of the design to form numerous loops, which are then cut to give a downy appearance. The skill is usually used to embroider the uppers of children's shoes and pillow slips. Embroideries made in this way can be seen everywhere in the countryside of North China.

Drawnwork has become an independent art form in embroidery with an exclusive set of skills. The material used includes plain-woven linen and cotton cloth. The method is to pull out some threads from the cloth in accordance with the chosen design and then tie the remaining threads with various stitches to form open work. The products include table-cloths, chair covers, handkerchiefs and clothing.

Pearl Embroidering (78) is otherwise known as Pearl Threading or Pearl Fastening. In this method, tiny pearls or glass beads are strung together, and the string thus formed is coiled and couched on the cloth to form patterns. The thread used should be very strong to withstand tension during sewing; the string is fastened as soon as it is coiled along the edges of the design. Where the string goes in a straight line, it is fastened regularly at intervals of eight or ten pearls. But where the string twists and turns, stitches are made behind every first or second pearl. Embroideries made in this way have a brilliant lustre. They are usually used for theatrical costumes, ladies' clothing and bags.

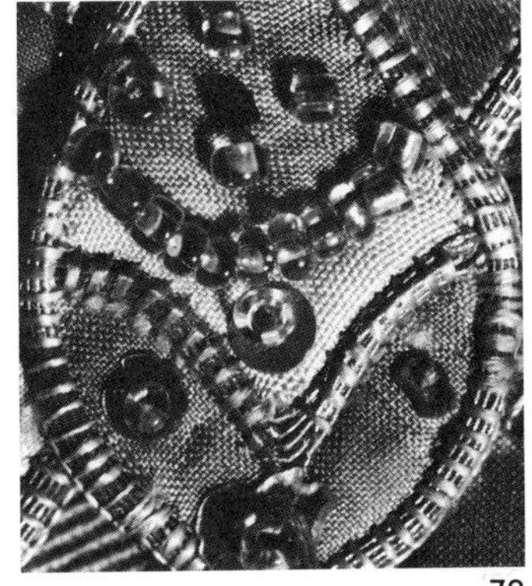
78

Spangle-fastening: gold foils or shining spangles (79) are often used in folk embroidery. Round or rectangular shiny pieces of metal help to brighten the design and add lustre to the work.

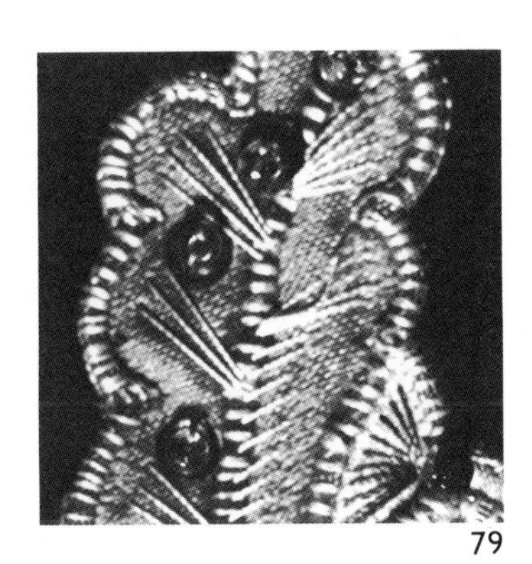
79

The Decorative Knot

The decorative knot is an ornament plaited with silk threads and attached to objects worn at the waist, like small bags and spectacle cases. There are many varieties. The few examples here include "the flat square knot" (80), "the long knot" (81), "the abacus bead" (82) and "the butterfly knot" (83, 84).

80

81

82

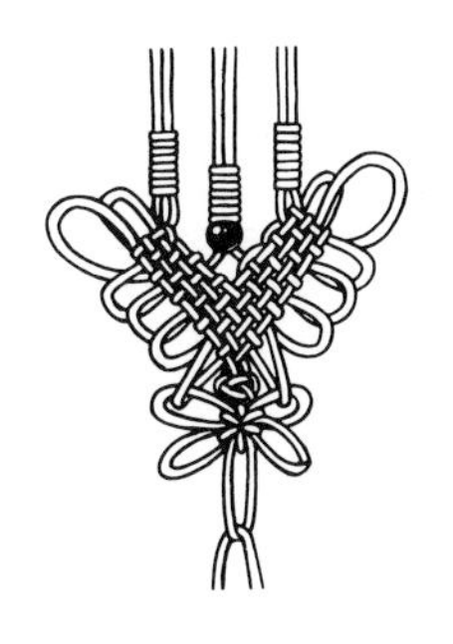
83

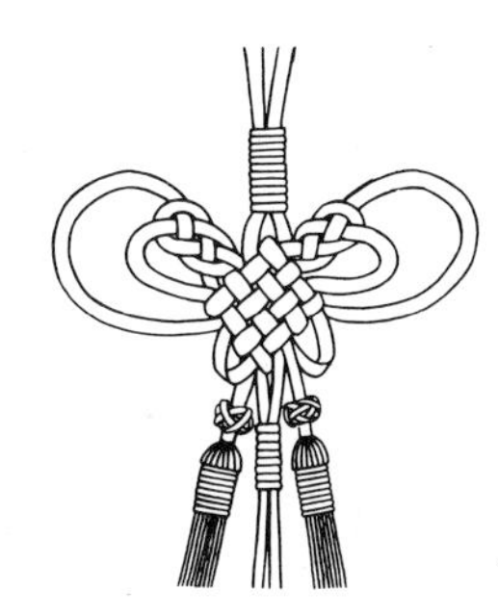
84

(C) Classification table of the main stitches used

Category	Stitch	Other Names	Earliest Specimen
Flat Stitchwork	Satin Stitch	Even, Straight, Beyond-the-edge	Found in a Western Han tomb at Mawangdui
	Vertical Satin Stitch		
	Horizontal Satin Stitch		
	Slanting Satin Stitch		
	Open Fishbone Stitch		An Eastern Han relic found at Nuoyinwula
	Spreading Stitch	Vertical, Horizontal, Slanting	
	Close-knit Stitch	Stick-in	Found in a Western Han tomb at Mawangdui
	Single Close-knit Stitch	Long-and-short	
	Double Close-knit Stitch		
	Multiple Close-knit Stitch		
	Layered Short-straight Stitch	*Qiang*	Tang Dynasty
	Inward Layered Short-straight Stitch	*Zheng Qiang*	
	Inverse Layered Short-straight Stitch	*Fan Qiang*	
	Mixed Straight Stitch	*Chan, Can, Souhe*	Southern Song embroidery *Riding a Crane over a Beautiful Terrace*
	Winding Stitch	*Rao*	Found in a Liao tomb at Yemaotai
	Pine-needle Stitch	*Basongmi*	Southern Song embroidery *Riding a Crane over a Beautiful Terrace*
	Wheel Stitch	*Bachegulu*	
	Scattering Stitch		Southern Song embroidery *Riding a Crane over a Beautiful Terrace*
	Vortex-like Pattern Stitch	*Shunxian*	
Embroidering of Lines	Stern Stitch	Rolling, Rod-like, Biting, *Bi*, Pulling, Willow	Southern Song embroidery *Riding a Crane over a Beautiful Terrace*
	Laced Back Stitch	*Biao*	
	Back Stitch	*Ji*, *Qie*, Back, Stabbing	Embroidered images of Buddha in Mogao Cave made in Northern Wei dynasty

Category	Stitch	Other Names	Earliest Specimen
	Running Stitch	*Gong*	
Couching	Couching of Silk Thread	Couching of Mixed Thread	Found in a Liao tomb at Yemaotai
	Couching of Palm Fibre		
	Couching of Horse-tail Thread		
	Quanjin (Quanyin)	Circling with Gold	Found in a Liao tomb at Yemaotai
	Pingjin (Pingyin)	Filling with Gold	Southern Song embroidery *Riding a Crane over a Beautiful Terrace*
	Fastening Stitch	Fixing	Southern Song embroidery *Riding a Crane over a Beautiful Terrace*
Pattern- shaping	Fur-simulation Stitch	Simulation, Realistic Fur Making, Fur Making	Found in Huang Sheng's tomb (Southern Song) at Fuzhou
	Eyebrow and Eyelash Stitch	*Bayanjiemao*	
	Binding Stitch	*Le*	
	Scale-laying Method	*Qianglin*	
	Scale-forming Method		Found in the Yuan ancient city of Jininglu
	Scale-piling Method		
Darning Embroidery	Darning Embroidery	*Purong* Embroidery, *Tiaoxiu*, *Pujin*, *Bierong*, Knitting Stitch	
	Lay-in Brocading	*Jiajin*, *Puyu*	Southern Song embroidery *Riding a Crane over a Beautiful Terrace*
Weave-in Embroidering	Gauze-embroidering	*Nasha*, *Kaidijin*, *Chuanhua*	Found in a Song tomb in Shanxi
	Chuosha		Found in a Song tomb in Shanxi
	Na Stitch		
Pulling Embroidery	Pulling Stitch	Lock Forming, Pulling Golden Lock, Winding-thread, Pulling and Winding Silk-locking, Coiling, Connecting	
	Double Pulling Stitch		
	Coiling Stitch		
Chain Embroidery	Chain Stitch	*Chuanhua*, *Taohua*, *Suohua*, *Luohua*, *Kouhua*, *Lahua*, Close-knit Stitch, Linking Stitch, Strands of Braids	Found in a Western Zhou tomb at Rujiazhuang, Baoji

Category	Stitch	Other Names	Earliest Specimen
	Close-ring Chain		
	Open-ring Chain		
	Double-ring Chain Stitch		
	Daisy Stitch	Detached Chain, Single-ring	Found in Chu tomb No.1 at Mashan, Jiangling
	Fly Stitch	Half-ring, Feather	Found in Chu tomb No.1 at Mashan, Jiangling
	Loop Stitch		Found in a Western Han tomb at Dabaotai
	Braid Stitch	Strands of Braids	
	Blanket Stitch	Edge-sealing, Sealing-the-openings, *Wenming* Edge, Button-locking	
	Suojin		
	Consecutive Stitch	Split	An Eastern Han relic found at Luobunaoer
Knotting	Knot Stitch	Making Knots, Knots, Ring Embroidering, Point	An Eastern Han relic found at Nuoyinwula
	Double Knot Stitch	Wheat Grain	
Netting	Net Stitch	*Huazhenxiu*, *Wenzhenxiu*, *Banhua*, Knitting	Southern Song embroidery *Riding a Crane over a Beautiful Terrace*
Tiaohua (picking patterns)	Cross Stitch	*Tiaohua*, *Jiahua*, Strings of Crosses, *Tiaoluo*, *Laling*, *Piehua*	An Eastern Han relic found at Nuoyinwula
	Open Fishbone Stitch		
Edging	Hound's-tooth		
	Lattice Pattern		
	Cucumber		
	Trellises		
	Lotus Leaves		
	Edge Sealing		
	Soujin		
	Edge Adding		

Category	Stitch	Other Names	Earliest Specimen
Others	Appliqué	*Buhua, Tiejuan, Tieling*	Found in Huang Sheng's tomb (Southern Song) at Fuzhou
	Baohua	Embossed Patterns	
	Piling Method	Padding, High-rising	
	Carving method	*Diaoxiu*, Hollowing-out, Edge-sealing	
	Random Stitch		Southern Song embroidery *Riding a Crane over a Beautiful Terrace*
	Double-face Embroidery	Two-face Embroidery, *Limianhua, Xianhua*	
	Shadow Embroidery	*Tuodixiu*	
	Ground-borrowing Embroidery	*Jiedixiu*	
	Colour-borrowing Embroidery	*Jiesexiu*, "Half-embroidery-half-painting"	Southern Song embroidery *Riding a Crane over a Beautiful Terrace*
	Gold-shadowing Embroidery	*Yinjin*	
	Core-wrapping Embroidery		
	Woollen-yarn Embroidery		
	Wool-cutting Embroidery	*Jianrongxiu*	
	Gerongxiu		
	Drawnwork		
	Pearl Embroidery	Pearl Threading, Pearl Fastening	
	Spangle-Fastening		Found in a Liao tomb at Yemaotai
Decorative Knot	Flat Square Knot		
	Long Knot		
	Abacus Bead		
	Butterfly Knot		

IV. APPENDICES

(A) Embroidery in Chaoyang District, Liaoning Province

by Wang Yarong

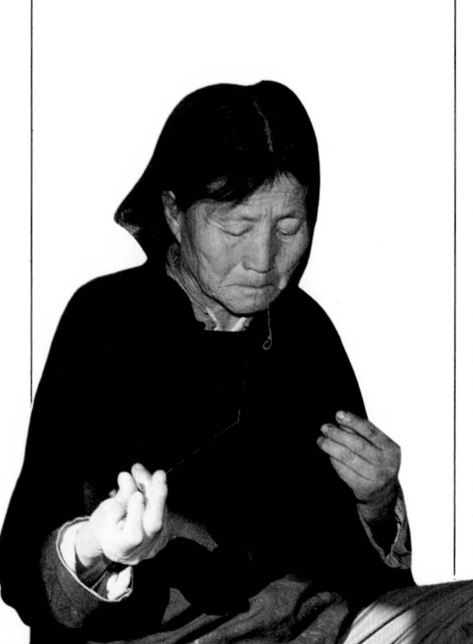

20. Li Dianzhi twisting a horse-tail thread

In November 1982 I took part in the excavation of Jin tombs, undertaken by the Liaoning Provincial Museum. This afforded me the opportunity to meet several folk embroidery artists, all women, living in Chaoyang County: Li Dianzhi, Mrs. Wei, and Zhou Zixian.

Fifty-eight-year-old Li Dianzhi was my landlady and a very warm-hearted woman. My interest in embroidery pleased her so much that she took the trouble to rummage through her chests and cupboards and found some old embroidered works of hers, such as a "butterfly pincushion" (see page 130), "purse with the design of old coins" (Illustration No. 21), a "Key-bag", and many others. She recalled in detail her keen interest in embroidery when she was a young girl, and the kinds of embroidery objects she had made. She even taught me some of the various techniques she used, such as twisting the "the horse-tail thread". As if by heredity, her daughter, Fengling, also loved embroidery. Embroidery objects of everyday use decorated with modern patterns filled the room. It is a shame that she used only one technique, *Jianrongxiu*, or Wool-cutting Embroidering (see page 146).

Accompanied by Fengling, I went to a remote mountain gully called Halahai where her grandmother lived. It was with great difficulty that we finally found Zhou Zixian, a master hand in embroidery well known throughout Chaoyang some decades ago. She was famous for her *purongnajin*, or Darning Embroidery (see page 137). Seventy-nine years of age, but still clear-minded and witty, she was a woman with an artistic disposition. Sadly this one-time master of embroidery had become totally blind. I owe much to this old woman for what I know about the folk embroidery in Chaoyang. She was very excited about my interest in her past career as an embroiderer and recalled with nostalgia the best embroideries she had made when she had been a girl and a bride and how they were appreciated by other people. She even told me of her method for handling silk thread, which she had formerly kept to herself: when embroidering with split silk threads, first pass the thread through a honey locust previously steeped in water before threading a needle. The thread will then look as if waxed. Embroidery objects using such threads will wear well and look smooth and shiny. If there is no honey locust, onions will also do. Perhaps this was the first time after so many years that she had had a willing listener ready to lend an ear to her talk about embroidery. She was especially pleased with me, even asking permission to run her hand over my face to know exactly what I looked like, so as to remember her "young friend". I was most willing to let her touch my face. Watching the pair of eyes which at one time must have been very bright, I was touched to tears. When I asked her whether she still kept any of her embroidered works, she told me regretfully that the last pair of pillow slips had been given to her second daughter when the latter got married. After a short pause, however, she took her walking stick and said, "Come on. Let's go to my second daughter's." Though the aged woman had not stirred out of doors for many years, and despite the icy wind, she did not hesitate to take me to a small village about ten *li* away, where her second daughter resided. Her daughter, who had been married for thirty years, had never used the treasured pillow slips until recently when her own son was about to get married. When I saw the fine embroidery pieces that she had done with her own hands (see Plate Nos. 102, 103), I could not help being filled with respect and love for this folk artist whom few people know. I was very lucky that day, for the old woman even succeeded in persuading her daughter to part with this last piece of embroidery when we left. She said that she felt more at ease with the pillow slips in my care, and that she wanted to make friends with me.

The experience remains vivid in my memory even today, as I recall my visit to Chaoyang, and I am very glad to take this chance to introduce my esteemed old friends and their works to the readers.

The following is a brief survey of the folk embroidery in Chaoyang. Most of the surviving famous embroidered works were done by local master needlewomen before their marriage and there are ample quantities for reference today. Following the custom prevalent in Hebei and Shandong Provinces, a girl in the locality when getting married was required to display a considerable number of embroidered works, which not only proved the bride's skill and cleverness, but became the best presents to her husband's relatives when she met them for the first time. These included door curtains (consisting of two kinds — "double *yaozi*" and "single *yaozi*", *yaozi* being a term which stands for the decoration, in single or double row, embroidered on the top end of the curtain; and *baohua* curtains (curtains with designs couched on them). These large pieces were hung at the door during festivals. They could also be hung on walls on ordinary days. Then there were embroidered "window curtains", "cupboard covers", "clock covers", "shoes", "key cases", "pin cushions", "scissors cases", "pouches for tailor's chalk lines", "table cloths", "pouches for needles and thread", "pillow slips" and many other embroideries which were used to decorate clothes, caps or to cover the mirror. There were also objects embroidered with the likenesses of characters in Chinese legends or in plays performed in the locality.

The embroidery technique used in Chaoyang consists mainly of satin stitching. But when the stitch is too long, the

21. Purse with a design of ancient coins, embroidered by Li Dianzhi

embroiderer will usually add an additional stitch in the middle or sew *Na* stitches, which do not run and wash well.

There are two types of embroidery — "monochrome" and "multi-coloured". Of the first type there are, for instance, blue curtains, the *yaozi* of which are made of patterns imitating the flowers of four seasons, all stitched in white (peony, water lily, chrysanthemum and plum in four bunches). White curtains are used only when a family is in mourning. As for multi-coloured embroideries, they are numerous.

Plied silk yarn is the chief type of thread used in embroidering. The local people call it "whole thread", while they call split floss "broken thread". In Chaoyang, silk floss split into four is the thinnest thread used. To twist a "horse-tail thread", a hair is taken from a horse's tail, and its end attached to that of a split thread. The free end of the split thread is then held between the teeth. The end of the horse tail hair connected to the split thread is held in the right hand and the other end in the left. Next the thread is twisted with the fingers of the right hand, with the left hand acting in unison. In this way, the split thread spirals around the whole length of the horse-tail hair. After that, a hard knot is tied at the end. The "horse-tail thread" thus made twists like the letter "Z". Another kind of "horse-tail thread" which twists in an "S" shape is made by pinning one end of the split thread on a quilt. A dark horse tail is suitable for a deep-coloured "horse-tail thread", and a white horse tail for a light-coloured one. "Horse-tail thread" is usually used to trim the edges of embroidered designs or to harmonize two strongly contrasting colours. The technique employed in trimming is the same as that used in couching.

The main stitch types used in Chaoyang number no less than thirteen. The designs on the embroidery articles are just as varied. Those on door curtains include the following: "Liu Hai scattering coins", "magpies perching on a plum branch", "fish swimming beside a water lily" (symbolizing harmony), "phoenix playing with a peony", and "lions playing with a silk ball". Couching is the usual technique used. Decorative articles like pillow slips are mostly embroidered with characters adorned with floral designs (Illustration No. 22). Other designs include "a hundred seeds contained in a pomegranate", * "happiness and longevity" (represented by coins), "phoenix facing the sun", "red plum with seeds", * "bamboo and its shoots", * "pine trees and cranes" (symbols of longevity), "two dragons playing with a pearl", and "unicorn tending its young". Flowers of the four seasons are also common themes. Objects with designs embroidered in relief include "ear muffs" and "pouches for tailors' chalk lines". Their designs are mostly done in the form of a triangular *ruyi* (an S-shaped symbol of good luck), a butterfly, a pup, a fish or a calabash. Embroideries done with couching techniques supplemented by stitching or painting represent another major type. Characters in Chinese legends symbolizing longevity and good luck are the themes usually used. The borders of embroideries are mostly decorated with motifs of "water ripple", "cucumber trellis", and others.

Whether in designs, colours or varieties, the embroidery in Chaoyang, is a distinctive type of folk embroidering art in North China, possessing many unique features, and is therefore worthy of our research and study.

January 1985
(Translated by Shi Huiqing)

---

* All symbolize offspring in plenty.

22. Pillow slip embroidered with characters adorned with floral designs

(B) The Embroidering Career of My Grandmother

by Wuliangai Suhe

The embroidered images of Buddha shown on the following two pages (Illustration Nos. 24, 25, 26) were done by my grandmother. Though they cannot show the full range of her skills, they nevertheless show the unique style of Mongolian embroidery.

My grandmother was born in 1860 into a distinguished family in Wengniute District. Her family name was Baoerjigude and her given name Cailajina (Illustration No. 23). She died in 1949. She was intelligent and dextrous when still a child. As she grew up, she began to learn needlework with her mother. At first she learned sewing but later she concentrated on the study of Mongolian traditional embroidery. The boots, pouches and small bags she embroidered in her teens were already admired for their ingenious design and fine workmanship. Her marriage with my grandfather was an extremely happy one. My grandfather, Yixizhongnai, was a scholarly man, versed in the Mongolian, Tibetan and Chinese languages and especially good at painting and calligraphy. His large collection of Chinese paintings and calligraphies contributed to the development of my grandmother's embroidery art. A table plaque embroidered with natural scenery which she made at that time really represents the peak of her achievement. This piece of work, 133 centimetres long and about 100 centimetres wide, was embroidered with hills, streams, buildings and human figures in colour on a white ground — mountains rising one above the other, jagged rocks, clouds and streams dimly discernible, numerous figures in various postures — the larger ones are less than an inch in height, while the small ones appear like so many ants, yet all possessed of distinctive features. Although the work seemed, at first glance, to imitate the style of traditional Chinese landscape painting it reminded one strongly of the great grasslands, for the red glaring sun, the wild geese flying high in the sky and

23. The late Qing Mongolian folk embroiderer Baoerjigude Cailajina

the flocks of deer, sheep and horses grazing in the valley were all embroidered with traditional Mongolian techniques. It is a pity that the work has now decayed. It can no longer be restored to its former splendour from the few fragments still in our possession.

The Mongolian people, being devout believers in Lamaism, regard the worship of Buddha as a major event in daily life. In our house, there was a special hall where we used to hold services in honour of Buddha and in which there were several pictures of Buddha embroidered by my grandmother along with the clay and wooden images. I was then only a small child and did not comprehend such things. But I still remember clearly what my grandmother told me about the hardships involved in embroidering a Buddha image. She must first of all undergo a period of fasting, then put up the embroidery frame in a quiet room, wash her hands and burn incense. Before she began embroidering, she would draw the sketch with the extinguished incense stumps. Except for the prescribed rules as regards the image of Buddha to be embroidered, she was free to choose the designs and colours for the accompanying scenes and objects. This required a high level of skill and artistic taste. Each Buddha image would take her at least a couple of months to complete, and sometimes this could be as long as six months or one year. These products of her painstaking labour are actually the treasures of our Mongolian embroidery art.

My grandfather died early, leaving my grandmother a widow in her middle age. Then she had the misfortune to lose my father, her only son. My brother and I were the only offspring who still lived with her. From then on, she was kept busy by housework and no longer took any interest in embroidery. These three images of Buddha are all that she has left behind her. Now, after a lapse of more than one hundred years, I can say with satisfaction that we have succeeded at last in preserving these embroideries in spite of difficulty. Before her death in 1949, my grandmother entrusted them to my wife Shumin, who took good care of them despite the poverty of the family, so that they were kept in good condition. During the Cultural Revolution, our house was repeatedly ransacked. But my wife had them sewn into our clothes so that they were able to escape destruction. Moreover, the embroideries now appear just as fresh in colour as when they were first made, even though they were often crumpled and wetted by perspiration in those years of trouble. It is indeed a great pleasure that we are able today to dedicate these precious specimens of Mongolian embroidery art to the public.

April 1984
(Translated by Shi Huiqing)

24. Image of Zongkaba, the founder of new Lamaism, executed in the Mongolian style (preserved by Suhe)

25. Mongolian-style religious picture (preserved by Suhe)

26. Mongolian-style religious picture (preserved by Suhe)

Postscript

Ten years ago, I was fortunate enough to be taught about Chinese ancient costumes and embroidery by Mr Shen Congwen. I frequently participate in excavating and studying ancient relics. During these activities, I often come upon some exquisite pieces of embroidery by folk artists, and I am especially fond of the small, functional articles, which I can admire and study for a long time without having the heart to part with them. These small pieces of embroidery were usually made by newly married women or girls reaching the marriageable age, manifesting their feelings and their longing for a happy life in their work. Made mostly for decorative purposes or to be given as gifts to friends and relatives, they were exquisite in workmanship and were especially appreciated and cherished by their owners. This explains why they were so well preserved and now we have the chance to see them with our own eyes. As these embroideries were made with the traditional techniques of Chinese folk embroidery in stitching, colour-blending and designing, they provide material for us to learn from and study. Besides, they help us to get a general idea of the development of Chinese folk embroidery techniques after we have consulted the great quantities of embroidered relics excavated. I therefore venture to dedicate this book, the result of my studies, to my teachers and those who share my interest. At the same time, I take delight in presenting my readers with pictures of some of my favourite embroideries for them to view and admire.

I owe much to Mr Shen Congwen for his teaching and guidance. Despite his great age and poor health, Mr Shen edited this book. I also want to thank Mr Wang Xu for his valuable help. This book records the results of their teaching efforts.

I should like to avail myself of the chance to express my gratitude to Mr Zhang Zhenheng and Mr Fu Xuiling for their support and assistance. Thanks are also due to Guangdong Provincial Museum, Zhongshan University at Guangzhou, Nanjing Museum, Hunan Provincial Museum, Jiangling Museum, Liaoning Provincial Museum, the Central Arts and Crafts Academy, Office of Historical Relics of Zhaowuda League of the Inner Mongolia Autonomous Region, Beijing Antique Shop, Mr Li Keyu, Mr Qi Congwen, and Mr Suhe for their information and materials. Lastly, I extend my heartfelt thanks to the editors of the Commercial Press (HongKong), who have made possible the publication of this book.

(Translated by Shi Huiqing)